FRA ANGELICO

The Light of the Soul

Painting panels
and Frescoes
from the Convent of San Marco,
Florence

by
Jacqueline and Maurice Guillaud

GUILLAUD EDITIONS / PARIS - NEW YORK
CLARKSON N. POTTER, INC. / NEW YORK
DISTRIBUTED BY CROWN PUBLISHERS, INC.

All of the photographs in this volume were taken by Nicolò Orsi Battaglini especially for us and to our specifications. To him go our heartiest thanks for his cooperation and his extremely painstaking work. We are indebted to Giorgio Bonsanti, Director of the San Marco Museum, for permission to publish these photographs, the first to show the frescoes in the Convent of San Marco since they were recently restored.

Assistant: Claude Le Cleach
Translators: Eleanor Levieux for the texts by Maurice Guillaud and the text by Giorgio Bonsanti on Missal n° 558. Dianne Dwyer for the text by Giorgio Bonsanti on the restoration of the frescoes of San Marco. The texts of the Old and New Testaments are taken from the King James version of the Holy Bible.
Editorial manager: Margot Feely
Editorial consultant: Mary Laing

First published by Guillaud Editions, Paris-New York, July 1986
Manufactured in Italy

Published by Clarkson N. Potter, Inc., 225 Park Avenue South, New York, New York 10003 and represented in Canada by the Canadian MANDA Group
Clarkson N. Potter, Potter, and colophon are trademarks of Clarkson N. Potter, Inc.

Library of Congress Catalog Card Number: 86-12359
ISBN 0-517-56340-1

Designed by Maurice Guillaud

Cover: Musician angel, Linaiuoli Triptych (detail)

previous page, fig. 1: San Pietro Martire Triptych (detail)

fig. 2: Page of Missal n° 558, c. 1430 (detail)

Table of Contents

Unless otherwise noted, all text by Maurice Guillaud.

Fra Angelico's Work in the Convent of San Marco, Florence

When, at Easter time in 1972, we undertook the "Angelican" pilgrimage — as we had each time we came to Italy — we had no idea that our search for the painter through his work would take so long, nor that it would lead to our writing a book about it. (Each of our stays in Italy was devoted essentially to Italian painting and led us to the smallest and remotest villages; the first one dates from 1952, when we went about carefully armed with our Berenson).

It was in 1972 that we methodically photographed the frescoes at the convent of San Marco and, once back in Paris, we showed slides of them. This induced us to gather together all the published material we could find on this very special Florentine artist. We soon learned to call "Fra Angelico" by his real name, Fra Giovanni.

Gradually we explored his paintings in our own way, not as specialists but as art lovers. The disparity of his work was perplexing, until Sir John Pope-Hennessy's writings clarified the image of the "real" Fra Angelico for us. Gradually, with the help of his authoritative attributions, we came to recognize features and successive stages in the development of the artist's work, which covered nearly three decades.

The sparse biographical data which has come down over the centuries offers us no more than

fig. 3: North Corridor of the Convent of San Marco

probable landmarks, a basis for inference: entries in various ledgers (concerning the payment of sums owed for commissioned works); the dates at which the edifices for which they were intended (churches, chapels, oratories) are known or thought to have been built; the dates at which those who commissioned works took office or died.(See the brief biography on page 33.)

What is certain is that Fra Angelico's work was very well known even in his own day, and that throughout the entire Renaissance period it lost none of its luster and none of its influence over artists and art lovers.

Selecting Works for Analysis; Establishing Authenticity; Chronological Order

Since it was customary for master artists, in the first half of the fifteenth century, to execute commissions with the aid of their workshops, many young artists came to work with Fra Angelico, first at San Domenico in Fiesole, where he continued to paint until the early 1440s, then at San Marco in Florence. They came to learn and, in the process, painted this or that portion of a work in progress — and then sometimes signed the work as if they had done all of it.

As a result it is very difficult to determine, even today, in an age which likes to call itself purist and makes use of the most up-to-date means of scientific analysis, exactly what Fra Angelico did paint — in whole or in part — and did not paint.

Nonetheless, by analyzing patterns of composition, the colors used and the way recurrent features of his themes are handled, and by assessing the degree of inspiration, we can arrive at a selective approach to works which can be considered authentic. Fra Angelico was such an original spirit that even when we have finished analyzing and assessing, and we eliminate work of dubious attribution, what remains is still very substantial, very rich. Although always rooted in a traditional line of religious inspiration, it is imbued — like the work of any genius — with a quality that defies classification, an everlastingness unique in the history of art.

We have chosen to focus on San Marco: the paintings on wood housed in the museum, and the wall frescoes painted in the convent.

Our final choice was determined by the most recent information given us by Sir John Pope-Hennessy in July 1985, when we visited the convent and the museum and were able to ascertain at first hand the results of the very extensive restoration begun late in 1976. (See, on page 9, Dr. Giorgio Bonsanti's comments on the restoration work.)

Altogether we present here the ten frescoes (six of them are in the friars' cells, two in the upstairs corridor leading to the cells, and two on the first floor, in the cloister) and nine other paintings or groups of paintings, in addition to a selection of miniatures from the San Marco Missal (no 558) and the series of thirty-two small panels depicting scenes from the life of Christ.

To provide a complete view of Fra Angelico's œuvre would mean including paintings situated outside San Marco — such as the Annunciation in Cortona; the Coronation of the Virgin, in the Uffizi; or the frescoes in the Cappella Niccolina, in the Vatican (these will be included in the book we are now preparing on the Renaissance frescoes in the Vatican chapels). First, however, the paintings reproduced in the following pages constitute over half of Fra Giovanni's output. Second, the paintings at San Marco are of such historical importance and of such high quality that they can be considered fully representative of his art. Since they show clearly each stage in the evolution of his style, they provide a very complete view of his development.

When it comes to placing Fra Angelico's work in chronological order, there is considerable uncertainty and opinions have often varied widely. Generally speaking, however, we subscribe to the dating proposed by Pope-Hennessy. We also wish to acknowledge our indebtedness to the critical catalogue by Umberto Baldini (Rizzoli, 1970; Flammarion, 1973, now out of print); the material it contains has been extremely helpful.

Gothic and Renaissance in Florence

By focusing on the relationship between image and faith, we seek to demonstrate how Fra Angelico, a man of religion who was nurtured in the Gothic convention, gradually came to accept and even to embody the Renaissance movement which had been gaining ground in Italy ever since its beginning with Giotto, among others, around 1300.

At the beginning of the fifteenth century Florence was a genuine center of creativity, stimulated by the Medici, who intensively promoted artistic production by their commissioning of works of all kinds. In this context of feverish activity, architects, sculptors and painters were in constant contact, and their communication led to applications of a new philosophy, a new and scientific spirit, which exalted relationships based on the preeminence of man and on a more rational conception of man's place in the formulation of ideas and in the universal scheme of things. At the same time they sought a new definition of beauty that harked back to antiquity.

As an heir to Gothic culture and the Gothic tradition of art, with its static formalism, Fra Angelico — the perfect example of the militant defender of the faith — must have needed a very inquisitive spirit, intermingled with his innate creative genius, in order to integrate the tenets of the new movement into his religious

fig. 4: San Marco Altarpiece
(detail from the central panel)

6

mission without compromising the singleness of his inspiration.

Never were more moving transmutations of faith and devotion created in images — images that invite the viewer to meditation, thereby drawing him nearer to the divine.

As the years go by, Fra Angelico's works seem ever more fresh, ever more beautiful. For a long time, his powers of innovation were compared to those of Masaccio, as each artist strove in his own way to come to terms with the changes taking place in art and ideas.

The San Marco Altarpiece, 1438-40 (figs. 67 to 71), and the Bosco ai Frati Altarpiece 1450-52 (figs. 153 to 160) — surely influenced by Alberti's treatise on perspective, published in 1435 — are high points in a new conception of painting which grew and gained ground for a hundred years, giving rise to the great classic period of the Renaissance. From its sources, chiefly in Florence and other parts of Tuscany, it overflowed Italy and surged across the entire western world.

Words and Images

Wherever possible, we have placed the appropriate passages from the Bible opposite the works illustrating them. The frescoes are reproduced on onionskin paper in an attempt to re-create, both visually and in tactile terms, the unique radiance of the walls on which they are painted, for there Fra Angelico's paintings appear to quiver like skin.

We have adopted a special lay-out for pictures and words (the notes and "dialogues" written by Maurice Guillaud) so as to convey as fully as possible the mystical vibrations emanating from Fra Angelico's creations. This is no easy task in an age where the achievements of science and technology generally replace the impulses of faith by individual — and often desperate —

pragmatic attempts to realize the potential of man.

But does not every attempt by man to exceed his own limits and those about him constitute a leap forward, a leap toward the absolute?

Jacqueline and Maurice Guillaud

Notes on the Restoration of Fra Angelico's Frescoes in the Convent of San Marco, Florence

A full appreciation of the magnificent frescoes by Fra Angelico and his assistants in the cells and corridors on the second floor of the convent of San Marco is possible today, thanks to their restoration. Begun toward the end of 1975, this large-scale project was finished in the late spring of 1983 and presented to the public on June 11 of the same year. The second-floor restorations had been preceded by the restoration of the large *Crucifixion* in the Sala del Capitolo on the first floor, carried out in 1968. This last operation had been dictated by urgent necessity. Although the flood of 1966 did not directly affect the fresco, it did cause the appearance of certain salts dangerous to the conservation of the painting — so dangerous, in fact, that the large *Crucifixion*, whose surface was too fragile to permit its removal from the wall, would be lost today had not a new restoration technique involving the transformation of sulfates into carbonates been developed on that occasion. The technique in question, the use of barium hydroxide to change the sulfates into stable barium carbonate (a substance similar to the calcium carbonate that constitutes the original plaster), was also used on the second-floor frescoes. The technique has already been described in scientific publications[*], and need not detain us here. Suffice it to say for present purposes that it has been in practice for over a decade, and that the theoretical propositions have been confirmed by experimental results.

[*] *See, in particular, E. Ferroni, Restauro chimico-strutturale di affreschi solfatati, in Metodo e Scienza. Operatività e ricerca nel restauro, Florence, 1982.*

The condition of the frescoes varied. Some, especially those on the north side (immediately to the right of the staircase), were more seriously damaged than others. The wall on which these frescoes are painted, above the first-floor arcades, faces north, and it was exposed to the elements for several centuries before the closing in of the so-called St Dominic Cloister. It was, moreover, a rather thin wall that probably suffered from the run-off of rain water from the roof, obviously equipped with an inadequate drainage system. The cells affected, nos. 40-42, contain interesting frescoes, although they are not in my view by Fra Angelico himself.

Some frescoes on the east side, near the St. Antonino Cloister, were also damaged, probably as a result of the same drainage problem.

All of these frescoes showed appreciable surface damage, with considerable loss of paint, especially in certain colors such as the dark background hues where the original carbonation had not been sufficient to fix the paint. Common to all the frescoes in the cells were scratches and abrasions, the result of the convent's history; at times it had served as soldiers' quarters. The frescoes were also very dirty, with considerable deposits of atmospheric grime or soot, due in part to the open braziers used to heat the cells. Some frescoes had also been treated in the past with *beveroni*, a colloquial term for a mixture of organic substances — mainly eggs — which had been applied to revive the colors, and which had

The restoration of the second-floor frescoes was begun at the end of 1975 under the aegis of the then director of the Museum of San Marco, Professor Luciano Bellosi, and was entrusted to one of the most noted fresco restorers, Dino Dini. Government funds soon ran out, at which point Dr. Hanna Kiel, a German friend who had long been a Florentine by adoption, intervened. She suggested to Baron Hans Heinrich von Thyssen, already committed to the idea of financing an important restoration in

Florence, that he concentrate his efforts on the frescoes of Fra Angelico in San Marco. The generosity of Baron von Thyssen — on whom the city of Florence conferred the honor of the « Golden Florin » at the inauguration of the restored frescoes — made it possible for the work to be completed. It also made possible the replastering of the cells and corridors, using a fifteenth-century technique whose details are outside the scope of these notes.

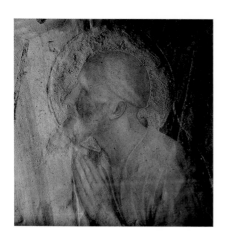 

Detail of the *Crucifixion* in the Sala del Capitolo, first floor, before restoration (left, showing sulfate crystals) and after (right).

The *Crucifixion with St Dominic*, cell 30: two details before restoration; the whole fresco after restoration.

subsequently caused them to yellow and darken.

The plan therefore called for cleaning, consolidation of the paint layer, and finally pictorial restoration. The following is a brief report on these three different phases.

The cleaning was carried out by Professor Dini, using the method most widely practiced; that is, the application of ammonium carbonate. This is not a solvent — since dissolving the dirt would cause it to penetrate even further into the plaster — but a gelatinous substance that brings the dirt to the surface, where it can then be washed off with distilled water. In order to act, the ammonium carbonate has to be applied with compresses consisting of several layers of Japanese paper (rice paper) or of wood pulp, in effect pure cellulose. Application by means of compresses also avoids friction, which is dangerous for the more delicate colors. The compresses are usually left on for several hours, in some cases up to twenty-four hours.

About two weeks after cleaning, as a rule, the consolidation of the paint layer is undertaken, using barium hydroxide as already mentioned. This is a delicate operation whose success depends basically on the method of execution, in particular on the relationship between the concentration of barium hydroxide and the length of time it is in contact with the painted surface. Normally a compress containing a 12 per cent concentration of barium hydroxide is left in place for seven to eight hours.

The final operation, that of pictorial restoration, calls for special comment. The work was carried out in accordance with the basic principles of the Italian school, codified in the restoration charter of 1972: the restoration must be reversible, and it must be discernible to the naked eye, without any investigative instruments or special techniques. At the same time the restoration must fulfill the fundamental purpose of rendering the contents of the painting

Restorer Dino Dini at work, removing the ammonium carbonate compress from the angel of the *Annunciation* at the top of the stairs.

Seen from inside, the compress after removal shows that dirt alone has been lifted.

The angel of the *Annunciation* emerges from cleaning.

In the same fresco, the area on the right, not yet cleaned, is in marked contrast to the part already cleaned.

In the *Transfiguration* in cell 6, the lower half has been cleaned; the color is still very wet and appears much darker than it will later, when dry.

intelligible as a whole, so that losses (such as a total absence of paint) or abrasions do not disturb the eye and prevent an overall appreciation of the work. Therefore, where there were isolated losses in the San Marco frescoes that interrupted the pictorial text, limited and recognizable restorations were carried out; earth colors similar to the originals were used in a water solution practically devoid of binder, so that they could be easily removed in the future, if so desired, with no danger to the original.

In some cases, there were special problems. Almost all of the frescoes had suffered from the construction of the barrel vault, which was not original and dated probably from a fairly recent period, possibly toward the end of the nineteenth century. The creation of this ceiling had caused damage to the upper parts of the frescoes, with actual losses of the *intonaco* — the final coat of plaster on which the frescoes were painted. These losses had been repaired by patching the plaster and restoring the paintings to imitate the originals. Impossible as

Detail of the Virgin's cloak in the *Annunciation* at the top of the stairs. Executed with azurite and badly damaged, it has been carefully "reintegrated"; the cooler tones mark the modern paint restoration.

Another example of paint restoration, limited to darkening the background; the missing area was too extensive for colors to be matched.

it is to imagine, however, in the cell with the fresco of the *Presentation in the Temple*, the loss of an entire piece of *intonaco*, with the painting of the marvelous shell-shaped niche revealed by cleaning, had led to the invention of an absurd red background for the whole composition.

The cleaning has also enabled us to recognize actual technical defects in the original, traceable to the painter himself. In the *Annunciation* of cell 3, for example, an insufficient percentage of binder made it impossible for the pigments to be absorbed into the plaster; as a result, the Virgin's robe is today completely transparent and almost colorless, revealing the beautiful preparatory drawing, laid down at high speed with a wet brush on the fresh plaster.

Two views of the *Presentation in the Temple* in cell 10 before restoration, and one after.

In other cases, cleaning has revealed a fresco very different from the one to which we were accustomed. In the *Adoration of the Magi* (Cosimo de' Medici's cell 39), the ground had been embellished with various grasses and plants, whereas Fra Angelico had designed it (the fresco was largely executed by an assistant) as bare and rugged. This fresco had been completely repainted, causing serious concern about the existence of the original paint underneath; this, however, was perfectly preserved. Let me add that although the decision to

The gown of the Virgin in the *Annunciation* in cell 3, after restoration.

Detail of the *Adoration of the Magi* in cell 39, after restoration; the Virgin's cloak has lost its color but retained the modeling.

remove the extremely banal blue in which the Virgin's cloak had been repainted did not lead to the recovery of the original color, almost entirely vanished as the probable result of an original technical error, it did disclose a legible trace of the fifteenth-century modeling, definitely preferable to the repainting.

Let us now turn to the historical and artistic consequences, in particular to certain observations and considerations that, as a result of the restoration, can today be stated with greater certainty. The first point to be considered is the organization of the work and the way in which it was laid out and executed by Angelico and his assistants. It appears clearly enough that the frescoes executed by Angelico himself are basically those on the outer side of the east corridor; that is, those in cells 1 through 10, together with the three on the corridor walls (the *Annunciation* at the head of the stairs, the *Crucifixion* immediately to the left of the entrance, and the "mural polyptich" known as the "Madonna of the Shadows" on the inner side of the east corridor). I remain a little doubtful about the frescoes of the Crucifixion in cells 41 through 43. All of the other frescoes seem to me to have been executed by assistants basing their work on exact drawings (even perhaps on the *sinopias,* the actual preparatory underdrawings done on the plaster before the *intonaco* is applied), for which Fra Angelico was undoubtedly responsible. Two possible explanations come to mind for this division of labor. One is that the project was very rapidly executed, with Angelico working on his thirteen frescoes while assistants carried out the others at the same time and under his direct control. The other is that Angelico's work was interrupted, possibly by his departure for Rome in 1445, and was carried on by others during his absence. My own inclination is in favor of the first theory: on the one hand, because we know that when the new church was dedicated at the beginning of 1443, Pope Eugenius IV slept in Cosimo de' Medici's cell, and it is difficult to believe that this had not been provided with its fresco (a fresco undoubtedly painted by assistants of Angelico, though without his direct intervention); and on the other, because actively engaged among these assistants was Benozzo Gozzoli, who is known to have also worked with Angelico in Rome and Orvieto. It is conceivable, therefore, that when Angelico went to Rome, most of the decoration had been finished, with one certain exception and possibly others. The certain exception is the "Madonna of the Shadows" fresco, which in my view is definitely later than the rest and can be dated to Angelico's return to Florence in 1450. The possible exceptions are the frescoes in cells 41 through 43; even if done by assistants, they seem to reflect coloristic experiences that belong to a later phase.

Detail, before and after restoration, of the *Agony in the Garden* in cell 34, attributed to Benozzo Gozzoli after Fra Angelico's design.

More important still are the effects of the restoration on the way in which we assess Fra Angelico's works within the stylistic evolution of the Renaissance. We must remember that until a few decades ago, Angelico was regarded as fundamentally a Late Gothic painter, whose decidedly archaic art constituted — in the Renaissance and in the mid-fifteenth century — a residuum from earlier periods, by then stylistically outdated, at least in Florence. A more accurate understanding of the great role played by Angelico in the Renaissance has developed relatively recently, due mainly to the exhibition of 1955. In my view, however, it is thanks to the restoration of the San Marco frescoes that the painter's exceptional contribution to the development of fifteenth-century Italian art can now be fully and clearly understood. In fact, Fra Angelico appears more and more as Masaccio's greatest interpreter and successor, and one of the most formidable exponents of the new art and its conquests: the sense of space; the taste for investigating the unknown; the unprejudiced way of confronting reality; and the wish to discover, explore and establish mathematical laws in order to render three-dimensional space on a flat surface by means of perspective. The restoration now shows in particular the volumetric force and power, the three-dimensionality with which Angelico was able to depict bodies; the colors have recovered, besides their transparency, their thickness; rather than staying on the surface like a simple pictorial film, they seem to have penetrated into the plaster. The yellows and reds, drawn from Masaccio's palette, and the search into the means of constructing figures (not merely defining them in independently realized outlines) constitute the most direct precedent for Piero della Francesca, and through him for the northern variants — Venetian and Lombard — of his art.

The *Mocking of Christ* in cell 7, before and after restoration.

Thus, for twenty years, in the fourth and fifth decades of the fifteenth century, Fra Angelico was the most important painter in Western art. The restoration of the San Marco frescoes is not only a joy for visitors' eyes but also a magnificent historical and critical operation, which has at last reconstructed an essential, and hitherto largely hidden, chapter of the Renaissance.

Giorgio Bonsanti

Director of the Museo di San Marco, of the Gallerie dell' Accademia, and of the Ufficio e Laboratorio di Restauro della Soprintendenza di Firenze.

Detail of the *Coronation of the Virgin* in cell 9, before and after restoration.

Missal 558, from the National Library in Florence (presently at the San Marco Museum)

This is the most important manuscript in San Marco's very rich collection. Unsigned, it consists of 156 parchment pages, with 104 additions; the format is 47.5 × 33.7 cm. It includes 30 miniatures and numerous illuminations and initial letters. Its margins have been trimmed. Like any missal, it comprises hymns, passages for reading, and prayers, and lays down the ritual for celebrating mass.

It is the only manuscript virtually all of whose miniatures can be attributed to Beato Angelico; this opinion was put forward in the nineteenth century and has been strongly upheld since the 1950s, chiefly by Mrs. L. Collobi Ragghianti and Mr. L. Berti. Only a limited number of the miniatures show traces of work by other artists — and indeed it is probable that they can be attributed to only one man, Zanobi Strozzi. It would seem that the manuscript could be dated from approximately 1430, when Beato Angelico was a friar at the Convent of San Domenico da Fiesole.

Some of the scenes remind us of others that were painted, in larger formats, on wood or as frescoes. Among the most remarkable are *Christ calling Saints Peter and Andrew*, the *Presentation of the Infant Jesus in the Temple*, the magnificent *Annunciation*, and *St Peter Martyr Being put to Death*. The angel in the *Annunciation* flies down through the air, rather than coming on foot, and the edges of his robe curl in on themselves as it streams about him; these two "clues" lead us to assign a fairly early date to the manuscript and to believe that Fra Angelico may have been trained in the workshop of a miniaturist close to that of the great Lorenzo Monaco (who died in 1425).

Some of these miniatures are surprisingly well preserved and gleam with gold and bright colors. Unfortunately this is not the case with the *Glory of St Dominic*, a.c. 67 v., one of the key pieces in this ensemble. In it, the artist blends the delicacy and the highly ornate quality inherent in miniatures with a breadth of conception and a sense of structure, combining to create the impression of a far larger and indeed monumental work.

(following pages)

figs. 5 to 13: Pages and details of Missal n° 558

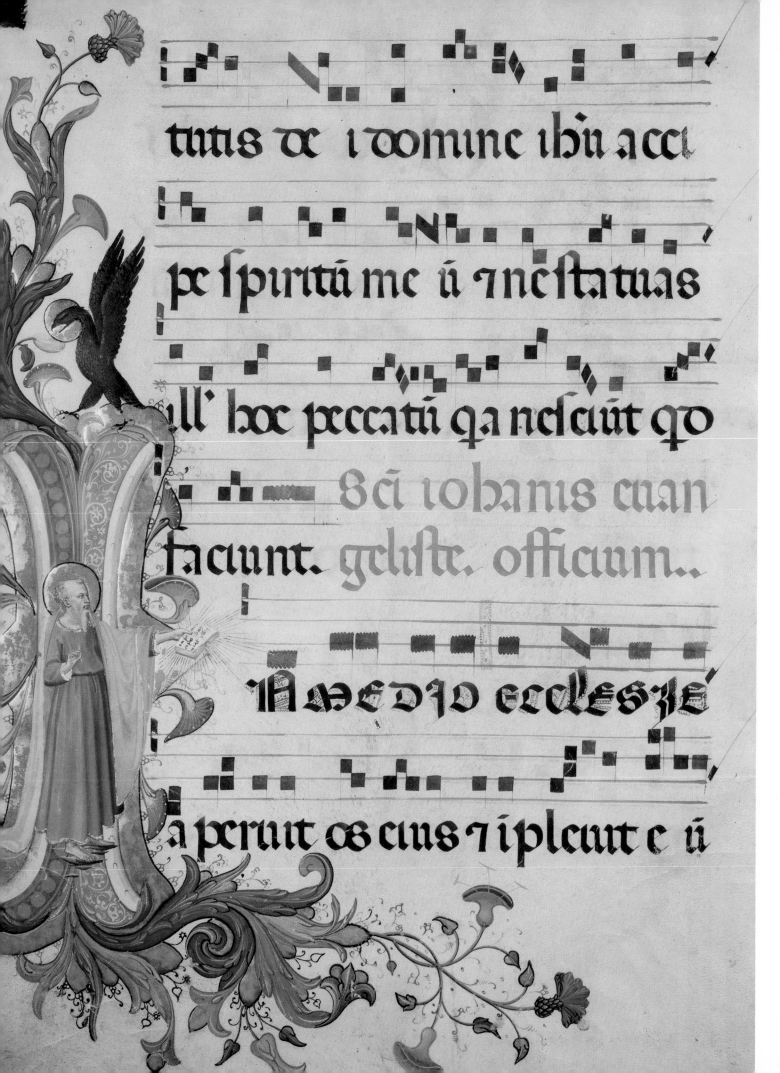

tutis dz i domine ihu acci

pe spiritu me u i ne statuas

ill' hoc peccatu qa nesciut qo

faciunt. Sci iohanis euan geliste. officium..

In medio ecclesie

a peruit os eius i i pleuit e u

orate ce li de
su per i nu
bes pluit iu
stu a periatur terra et ger
tp̄.
minet saluatorem. rẽs. alle
luya. alle lu ya. ꝟ. Et iu

Fra Giovanni, Called "Fra Angelico"
A Brief Biography

The Early Years : Fiesole

The painter we know as Fra Angelico was born
Guido di Piero, sometime between 1395 and
1400, somewhere in Tuscany, in the province
of Florence.

Very early in life he was taught the art of painting miniatures. He was still known only as
Guido di Piero when he painted his earliest
works, among them an altarpiece for the
Gherardini chapel of the church of Santo
Stefano al Ponte in Florence (1418). In about
1420 he became a Dominican friar, entering

fig. 14: The Convent of San Domenico da Fiesole

the community of *San Domenico da Fiesole*, on the hill that overlooks Florence. It was then that he was given the name of *Fra Giovanni*, and became known to his contemporaries as *Fra Giovanni da Fiesole*.

For nearly twenty years he painted in his studio at *San Domenico*, while pursuing his life as a friar. In 1432 and 1433, and again at several other times until 1436, he held the position of vicar in the Fiesole community.

San Marco

San Marco, Fra Angelico was placed in charge of providing the pictorial decoration for all of them and of producing a large altarpiece for the church. He seems to have maintained his studio at *San Domenico* until 1440, although by that time work on the *San Marco Altarpiece* was already well advanced and the frescoes in the convent had begun. The first indication of his presence at *San Marco*, where he moved his studio, dates from 1441.

Until the end of 1445 Fra Angelico devoted

In 1436, a papal bull issued by Eugenius IV assigned the premises of the Silvestrine convent of *San Marco* in Florence to the Dominicans of Fiesole. Fra Angelico was not among the friars who took possession of *San Marco* in the same year, but stayed on in Fiesole as vicar. In 1438, however, when Michelozzo began his reconstruction of the buildings at

fig. 15: The Convent of San Domenico da Fiesole

himself to his work at *San Marco*, designed as it was to stimulate the brothers in their lives of contemplation and prayer. The frescoes that can be attributed solely to him are those in cells 1, 3, 6, 7, 9, and 10; the *Christ on the Cross Adored by St Dominic* in the cloister, facing the entrance; the large *Crucifixion* in the *Sala del Capitolo*, or chapter house; the

fig. 16: The Convent of San Marco

large *Annunciation* and the *Virgin and Child Enthroned with Eight Saints* in the upper corridor. For all the other paintings, in which his pupils and assistants took part, it was Fra Angelico who created the overall plan. This accounts for the great degree of conceptual unity among all the San Marco frescoes.

In 1443 Fra Angelico was appointed *sindico,* that is, manager of the community, in charge of all transactions on the friars' behalf.

First Stay in Rome (1445-50)

In 1445, Pope Eugenius IV, who was familiar with Fra Angelico's work, summoned him to Rome. Soon after the painter arrived, the pope, it is said, offered him the post of archbishop of Florence, for that seat was vacant; but apparently Fra Angelico refused it and recommended Fra Antonino Pierozzi, vicar of San Marco, instead. Fra Antonino was indeed made archbishop.

During his years in Rome, Fra Angelico and his assistants decorated the chapel of San Pietro in the Vatican. He also carried out frescoes for the chapel of St Nicholas, which was later destroyed, and decorated the Cappella Niccolina in the Vatican. In the summer months of 1447, he began work on the frescoes in the San Brizio chapel in the cathedral of Orvieto, leaving his pupils to complete them.

Return to Florence

In about 1450 Fra Angelico returned to Fiesole, where he stayed for three or four years, this time as prior of San Domenico. It was during this period that the oratory of the Santissima Annunziata in Florence was roofed over, dating the commission for the *Scenes from the Life of Christ,* which were painted for its silver chest.

Second Stay in Rome

Fra Angelico returned to Rome sometime in 1453-54, but we have no indication of any work he may have carried out during the period. He died in Rome in 1455 and is buried in the church of Santa Maria sopra Minerva.

In addition to his frescoes, a fairly limited number of panel paintings have survived; most of them are now in the Museum of San Marco in Florence.

Fra Angelico developed a modern pictorial language. Little by little he shook off the Gothic conventions, using color and space in innovative ways. In a manner uniquely mystical and his own, and with a total commitment to his spiritual vision, he gave expression to the new movement — the *rinascimento* — of his time.

fig. 17: **The Convent of San Marco**

36

The San Pietro Martire Triptych

In 1429, an entry in the ledger of the San Domenico convent in Fiesole recorded that the Camaldolese nuns of the order of San Romualdo, in San Pietro Martire, owed the

sum of 10 florins for an altarpiece commissioned from Fra Giovanni. It was the rule that payment for work done by any member of a Dominican congregation went straight into the community coffers.

fig. 18: San Pietro Martire Triptych, 1428-9. Panel painting 137 × 168 cm

Although there was once doubt about attributing any part of the altarpiece to **Fra Angelico**, it is now generally agreed that this is an authentic example of his work. If we examine illuminations by him (figs. 5 to 13), we find that the expressions on the faces of figures in the *San Marco Missal* miniatures are similar to those in the scenes painted between the pinnacles of the triptych.

The Annunciation was a theme that **Fra Angelico** was to handle often and superbly; indeed it is one of the major themes of the Christian liturgy. Here, although its protagonists (figs. 25 and 26) are more than three feet apart, they are in close communication; **Gabriel** leans forward with intensity. Above them, in the center medallion, is **God the Father** (fig. 22), whose gesture also takes in

fig. 19: **San Pietro Martire Triptych** (detail) **The Preaching**

the Virgin and Child below him.

The three pinnacles are linked by two very handsome scenes from the life of **St Peter Martyr** which add considerable interest to the triptych (figs. 19 and 20). The two episodes are narrated with great animation, a departure from the stark and remote style of traditional religious paintings; their colorful movement offsets the style — still very **Gothic** — of the three main panels and the gables, painted against a gold background. In the two upper corners are trees but no figures; they balance a composition in which the two pairs of saints balance and complete each other. There are no predella panels, suggesting that these paintings, which crown the work as a whole, were intended to replace them.

fig. 20: **San Pietro Martire Triptych** (detail) **The Martyrdom**

It is a pleasure to look at the two small scenes in detail. Both take place outdoors. St Peter Martyr (fig. 19) preaches in a village whose houses give depth and definition to the space. Painting one century after Giotto, Fra Angelico obviously had his own ideas on volumes and landscapes; these are quasi-realistic and make novel use of color. The saint is preaching from a pulpit high above the women seated on the ground, Oriental fashion. The men are standing; one of them gesticulates. A plump, white, elongated cloud adds a mystical note to the little scene, punctuated by trees with gold highlights in their foliage. In the martyrdom scene (fig. 20), nature is harsher, its steep lines and slopes very like those of Tuscany. The rock on the left, rising above the wooded valley, prefigures the often symbolic rocks which appear in Fra Angelico's later paintings, such as the great rock of the Holy Sepulchre in the *Noli Me Tangere* (fresco in cell 1, convent of San Marco, fig. 72). Peter, at death's door, writes on the ground in letters of blood, *Credo deu R* while his executioner readies the fatal stroke. The red garment of the executioner is almost symmetrical with that of the gesticulating man in the left-hand scene.

But the message of the triptych is of course embodied essentially in the six large figures who occupy the three main panels. The Virgin and Child (fig. 21) are flanked by four saints: on the right (fig. 26), Peter Martyr and Thomas Aquinas; on the left (fig. 25), John the Baptist and Dominic, carrying the lily.

Without creating an effect of genuine perspective, the artist has achieved a sense of depth, for the saints do not all stand along the same line: the inner figure of each pair is placed slightly to the rear. At the same time, a very clear difference of scale thrusts the Virgin's

fig. 21: Detail from the *San Pietro Martire Triptych* (Central panel)

throne into the foreground. The dark platform on which it stands makes the Virgin appear more majestic, an effect which is accentuated by the blue volume of her cloak.

The Child stands very straight on his Mother's knee. His air is somewhat pedantic: are we the doctors in the Temple? None of the figures has an expression of great spirituality.

One interesting aspect of this triptych is the relationship between the colored masses formed by the garments; the blacks and whites provide a strong rhythm, and are virtually symmetrical at either side of the painting. They stand out by contrast with the reds, which compete successfully with the blues and greens. The rich fabric covering the throne exemplifies a different way of handling gold.

San Pietro Martire Triptych (details)

fig. 22 : God the Father

fig. 23: The angel of the Annunciation

fig. 24: The Virgin

fig. 25: Saints Dominic and John the Baptist

fig. 26: Saints Peter Martyr and Thomas Aquinas

The Virgin and Child Enthroned

Except for the gable surmounting it, this painting is undoubtedly by Fra Angelico's own hand. It can be dated approximately 1428-30. It was traditional to use gold for the background; here however, we find gold employed no longer as a ground for the painting but as a color in its own right.

Already, in the San Pietro Martire Triptych (fig. 18), we have noted the special way in which the gold in the fabric draped over the Virgin's throne was handled. Here it is used again in the same way, but even more emphatically, hinting at what was to come in later works, where the handling of gold was gradually stripped of any trace of the Gothic spirit: we need only observe the curtains in the center panel of the Linaiuoli Triptych (fig. 38) and, an even better example, the rich fabric of the Virgin's throne and the great curtains framing the landscape in the background of the San Marco Altarpiece (fig. 67).

Here again, the Virgin's gown is of an intense blue; the gown clings to her knees, which appear to be enlarged and moved farther forward; while this effect makes her appear heavier, its contrast with her narrow shoulders and her face makes them appear still more slender. Although the face itself is very finely drawn, its expression can be said to be unconvincing.

The infant Jesus is very much present, on the contrary; keen-eyed and chubby-cheeked, he stands sturdily on his Mother's knees. His robe widens out at the bottom, and its distinct sculptural folds make his body with its outthrust chest appear longer.

The infant's very physical presence enables us, on second thought, to appreciate the spiritual quality of the Virgin's face. The contrast is characteristic of Fra Angelico's art, for he often sets off a relationship of immediate reality, sometimes of naturalistic expressiveness, against an impression of remoteness — as if he were rubbing out his figures. By so doing, he intensifies the sense of the divine and rejects direct narration in order to enhance the spiritual dimension of his subjects. (How could he make us feel the vibrations of the divine essence more truly, more intensely than by his handling of the Virgin and Jesus group in the Bosco ai Frati Altarpiece (fig. 153)? How utterly different it is from his handling of the saints in the foreground!).

fig. 27: Virgin and Child Enthroned, c. 1430
Panel painting 189 × 81 cm

The Last Judgment

When the Son of man shall come in his glory, and all the holy angels with him, then shall he sit upon the throne of his glory: And before him shall be gathered all nations: and he shall separate them one from another, as a shepherd divideth his sheep from the goats: And he shall set the sheep on his right hand, but the goats on the left.

Then shall the King say unto them on his right hand, Come, ye blessed of my Father, inherit the kingdom prepared for you from the foundation of the world: For I was an hungred, and ye gave me meat: I was thirsty, and ye gave me drink: I was a stranger, and ye took me in: Naked, and ye clothed me: I was sick, and ye visited me: I was in prison and ye came unto me.

fig. 28: Last Judgment (detail)

fig. 29: Last Judgment, c. 1431
Panel painting 105 × 210 cm

Then shall the righteous answer him, saying, Lord, when saw we thee an hungred, and fed thee? or thirsty, and gave thee drink? When saw we thee a stranger, and took thee in? or naked, and clothed thee? Or when saw we thee sick, or in prison, and came unto thee?

And the King shall answer and say unto them, Verily I say unto you, Inasmuch as ye have done it unto one of the least of these my brethren, ye have done it unto me. Then shall he say also unto them on the left hand, Depart from me, ye cursed, into everlasting fire, prepared for the devil and his angels: For I was an hungred, and ye gave me no meat: I was thirsty, and ye gave me no drink: I was a stranger, and ye took me not in: naked, and ye clothed me not: sick and in prison, and ye visited me not. Then shall they also answer him, saying, Lord, when saw we thee an hungred, or athirst, or a stranger, or naked, or sick, or in prison, and did not minister unto thee? Then shall he answer them, saying, Verily I say unto you, Inasmuch as ye did it not to one of the least of these, ye did it not to me. And these shall go away into everlasting punishment: but the righteous into life eternal.

Matthew 25, 31-46

This large painting (fig. 29) was executed in 1432-33 for the Order of the Camaldolese nuns of Santa Maria degli Angeli. What accounts for its strange shape? Most specialists now believe that it constituted the upper portion of the seat reserved for the priest celebrating sung mass, and that Fra Angelico actually took advantage of this structural obligation to contrive a clever distribution of the different scenes forming his subject. There

fig. 3o: Last Judgment (detail)

are many other examples of the artist's marked talent for adapting himself to the constraints imposed by the surfaces on which he painted: for instance, the *Santa Trinita Altarpiece* (fig. 131), where, on a panel inserted in a gilt frame of strictly Gothic style, he carried out one of his freest, most Renaissance compositions; or again, the sublime frescoes he painted in the cells of the convent of San Marco despite the narrowness of the space available.

It was thus within a very singular format that Fra Angelico resolved the problems inherent in the "staging" of the Last Judgment. The problems had to be faced by all those artists before him who had striven to depict religious subjects. The most sought-after effect was the dread inspired by the punishments of Hell, often given a very simplified treatment which at first glance may seem appropriate and which Fra Angelico here actually makes more appealing. At most, as Luciano Berti puts it, Fra Angelico makes his *Last Judgment* "a pious fable or a sermon". But in offering us a Heaven and an Earth that complete each other and a Hell and a Paradise that contrast with each other, he gradually reveals other sources of concern: Heaven dominates Earth — the lower realm — which is cut into two heterogeneous parts.

An extraordinary caesura, of both style and theme, occurs in the very center of the painting. It captures the viewer's attention from the first to such an extent that it overshadows all the other elements of the work.

It is in fact a thread that Fra Angelico gives us to guide us through his vision.

The break is not just an unbridgeable gap separating the two realms decreed by the Last Judgment, the realm of the damned and that of the elect.

It is a strange and terrifying space stretching on

fig. 31: Last Judgment (detail)

and on almost to the horizon. It is what remains of the world once all human society has come to an end. It is an enormous cemetery, the product of human folly and human sin.

The trumpets of the Last Judgment have just sounded, wrenching open the tombs from which, minutes before, the risen — the good and the wicked — have emerged (fig. 32).

And I saw another angel fly in the midst of heaven, having the everlasting gospel to preach unto them that dwell on the earth, and to every nation, and kindred, and tongue, and people,

Saying with a loud voice, Fear God, and give glory to him; for the hour of his judgment is come: and worship him that made heaven, and earth, and the sea, and the fountains of waters.

And there followed another angel, saying, Babylon is fallen, is fallen, that great city, because she made all nations drink of the wine of the wrath of her fornication.

And the third angel followed them, saying with a loud voice, If any man worship the beast and his image, and receive his mark in his forehead, or in his hand, The same shall drink of the wine of the wrath of God, which is poured out without mixture into the cup of his indignation; and he shall be tormented with fire and brimstone in the presence of the holy angels, and in the presence of the Lamb: And the smoke of their torment ascendeth up for ever and ever: and they have no rest day nor night, who worship the beast and his image, and whosoever receiveth the mark of his name.

fig. 32: Last Judgment (detail)

Here is the patience of the saints: here are they that keep the commandments of God, and the faith of Jesus.

And I heard a voice from heaven saying unto me, Write, Blessed are the dead which die in the Lord from henceforth: Yea, saith the Spirit, that they may rest from their labours; and their works do follow them.

And I looked, and behold a white cloud, and upon the cloud one sat like unto the Son of man, having on his head a golden crown, and in his hand a sharp sickle.

And another angel came out of the temple, crying with a loud voice to him that sat on the cloud, Thrust in thy sickle, and reap: for the time is come for thee to reap; for the harvest of the earth is ripe.

And he that sat on the cloud thrust in his sickle on the earth; and the earth was reaped.

And another angel came out of the temple which is in heaven, he also having a sharp sickle.

And another angel came out from the altar, which had power over fire; and cried with a loud cry to him that had the sharp sickle, saying, Thrust in thy sharp sickle, and gather the clusters of the vine of the earth; for her grapes are fully ripe.

And the angel thrust in his sickle into the earth, and gathered the vine of the earth, and gathered the vine of the earth, and cast it into the great winepress of the wrath of God.

And the winepress was trodden without the city, and blood came out of the winepress, even unto the horse bridles, by the space of a thousand and six hundred furlongs.

Revelation 14, 6-20

fig. 33: Last Judgment (detail)

By using a device of which the proponents of Conceptual Art might be proud — by contracting into a single image an entire macrocosm of realities — Fra Angelico condenses into this one endless perspective of tombs, the dread, apocalyptic message of Revelation, making it echo in our imaginations.

The most significant aspect is the way he employs architecture to further narration. This is one of the great — and entirely modern — discoveries made by the early Italian Renaissance painters, from Giotto onward. In medieval imagery it was customary to call upon elements of man-made construction only to create a setting, a background. The Renaissance painters brought them on stage, as it were, as if they were human figures, giving architecture a key role in their pictorial creations.

We will not attempt to define architecture here, especially if we wish to include in it not only notions of rhythm, structure, and volume but also that of color. In Fra Angelico's *Last Judgment,* the two rows of abruptly opened tombs are treated monochromatically — actually, bichromatically, in black and white — and this makes the cleavage between them and the rest of the composition, with its vivid tones, even sharper. The focal point becomes the apocalypse itself, negation leading to nothingness.

Here, the original function of the "pious fable" becomes clear, a warning is given: "Be you good or be you wicked, do not forget the fate that awaits you all on earth." In a single image, the sarcophagus, placed squarely in the foreground, completes the parable of death. Once that statement is made, everything else in the narrative falls into place: the episodes depicted on either side are far from being naive repetitions of the traditional anecdotal imagery.

If we bear that in mind, we can find this composition quite captivating. Each zone is

fig. 34: Last Judgment (detail)

given a circular treatment, even the writhing mass of the damned at the gates of hell, about to be thrust into eternal fire and brimstone. Red and black are the dominant colors in this realm of the accursed (fig. 33). The arid rock of the infernal mountain, symbolizing destruction, is similar to that which encloses Christ's sepulcher in *Noli Me Tangere* (fig. 72); or the rock in the wonderful *Lamentation* from the predella of *San Marco*, now in Munich; or many others, typical of rocks found in Tuscany. Inside the mountain, officious demons prepare a broth of the damned for Satan's pleasure (fig. 34).

Some of the other torments displayed in this debonair Hell may make us smile — but they might have caused us to shudder if Fra Angelico had painted these scenes himself, or had decided to make the horror believable.

From the very dissimilar ways certain details are handled — particularly the faces, some expressive and some stereotyped, of the people who find themselves in Paradise or in the Garden of the elect — we realize that a number of pupils must have had a hand in producing this painting. As in so many other instances, it is difficult to know which parts of it can safely be attributed to the master himself. But that is of only minor importance; for in his overall concept Fra Angelico goes far — and takes us with him.

As a man of faith, he attempted, through his art, to enable us to approach God. The paths he followed in so doing were laid down by obedience to something more personal than the single ideal of beauty held up by the incipient Renaissance, although he did not deny that ideal. The means he used were original, intuitive, infinitely delicate, the tones comprising his melodic line sometimes surprising.

That is the case with this *Last Judgment*; although often considered a hybrid work, it is actually typical of an attempt, a vision which led the way to other conceptions of painting, beyond the purely narrative.

fig. 35: **Last Judgment** (detail)

The Linaiuoli Triptych*

A monumental work which can be dated from 1433-35, the Linaiuoli Triptych constitutes a turning point in Fra Angelico's career. In an original and masterful way he breaks away from the formal burden of Gothic structures, yet without rejecting their spiritual basis.

In terms of its overall design, this triptych corresponds to the various schemes which the Florentine sculptor Ghiberti put into practice with regard to volumes — their rhythm, their arrangement, and their decoration. There are strong grounds for believing that Ghiberti and his studio may have created the decorated marble pediment and frame of the triptych, and they may also have designed the two painted wings on either side of the central panel.

This masterly work was the result of a commission by the linen weavers' (linaiuoli) guild. In it, Fra Angelico brought together the boldest and most widely acknowledged trends of the new Renaissance movement, of which he was to be a pivotal figure, incorporating the utmost expression of humanistic values, opening the way to the modern age.

The monumental aspect of the marble framework for these painted panels takes us at first by surprise. We can then see clear evidence of the collaboration by Ghiberti, the creator of narrative sculpture, and his pupils — a reminder of the studio context in which the masters of the time produced their work.

It appears unlikely that the four saints on both sides of the folding wings (figs. 37, 39 and 40) were painted entirely by Fra Angelico. Although Saints John the Baptist and John the Evangelist (on the inside) and Saints Mark and Peter (on the outside) are imposingly tall and their garments display dazzling hues, they are not really convincing. Much later, Dürer was to paint these same saints and endow them with monumental presence. St Peter's face, with its expressive gaze and finely modeled features, was certainly painted by Fra Angelico, but the faces of the other saints do not "vibrate" in that uniquely Angelican way. One hand may have been responsible for the garments, and another, or others, for the faces.

The three panels of the predella give rise to fewer questions of attribution. They are eloquent expressions of religious inspiration, and the delicacy of their composition is consonant with the finest developments in the master's art.

The *Martyrdom of St Mark* (fig. 43) comes as a surprise, with its hailstorm; wind is still tossing the tree which stands out against a stormy sky (Pope-Hennessy finds some analogy with the *Miracle of the Snow* by the Sienese painter Sassetta). The people begging for mercy on the right form a dramatic and extremely realistic group. Similar realism had already been achieved with the small figures in the scenes of the San Pietro Martire Altarpiece (figs. 18 to 27). The three witnesses, forming a corresponding group on the left, convincingly express their protests. Like a long black hyphen, the martyr's body links the two sides of the painting. In the

fig. 36: Last Judgment (detail)

* 1433-5 Panel painting 330 × 260 cm (open)
330 × 168 cm (closed)

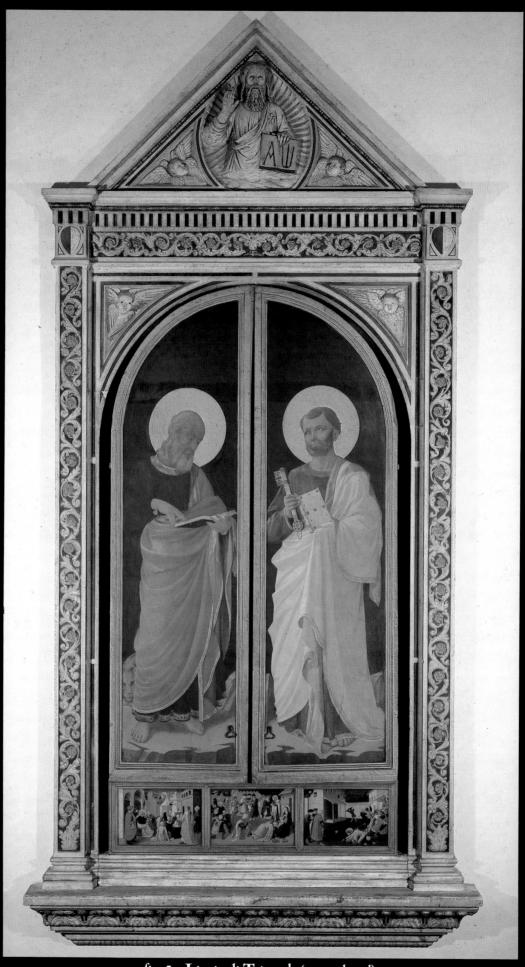

fig. 37: Linaiuoli Triptych (wings closed)
Saints Peter and Mark

fig. 39: Linaiuoli Triptych
St John the Baptist (inner side of the left wing)

70

fig. 40: Linaiuoli Triptych
St John the Evangelist (inner side of the right wing)

upper left-hand corner, the angel bearing his message adds a contemplative note. The architectural features, well articulated spatially and well balanced, strengthen the overall composition even though it revolves around an empty center. What pupil would have been capable of doing what Angelico manages in this handsome work: contrasting the exterior world of action with the world of prayer and faith? The martyred saint is the embodiment of tranquillity even as he is being dragged along the ground.

In another panel, *St Peter Dictating the Gospels of St Mark* (fig. 41), Fra Angelico achieves a sort of allegretto; a very free and polyphonal effect suffuses the houses, the city as a whole, and the small throng that fills the center of the composition. The rhythms of the varicolored walls and arcades are as musical as the figures themselves in their non-static arrangement, lightly or strongly accented, providing a counterpoint to the strong architectural volumes. This composition also revolves around a central point, St Peter's pulpit.

The center panel of the predella, the *Adoration of the Magi* (fig. 42) is yet another circular composition; but this one is stabilized, focused on the encounter between the tribute-offering king and the newborn Infant. The decorative nature of this work suggests that Fra Angelico's pupils had a hand in it. But the initial design is certainly by the master himself: there is a clear rhythm to the whole, especially in the robes, cloaks and other garments. The modeling of the faces — particularly those of the two men facing us in the group of three in prayerful discussion, on the left — is noteworthy.

The great central panel of the triptych (233 × 133 cm) is monumental in size and handles its subject, the Virgin and Child, in totally new ways. Beyond a doubt, it is the first great

summit in Fra Angelico's art.

The draped curtains on either side are full of movement; they stand out against a night-blue sky punctuated by regularly spaced golden stars, where the dove of the Holy Spirit hovers.

The folds of the Virgin's gown fall more freely than heretofore; they are distinct and weighty in a realistic way, without the stiffness of Gothic convention.

We have already seen how gold can be used as a color. In this rich fabric and these sumptuous brocades, gold is everywhere; the yellows blended with it make it all the more magnificent. The artist-friar pays tribute to his God, using every means at his disposal to express his faith.

Such an abundant display of fabrics is probably an indirect tribute as well to the members of the linen weavers' guild, who had commissioned the triptych.

Jesus stands on one foot on his Mother's knee; an animated figure, he gives us his blessing. Is he perhaps speaking to us? The Virgin, as so often, is a restrained presence, lost in contemplation of her Infant-God (fig. 44). In the foreground, the painted "marble" inlays at the base of her throne add to the richness of the setting.

A narrow strip (15 cm) enlivened by twelve angels arches over the center panel. Here Fra Angelico's use of forms and colors brings to mind, even more irresistibly than before, a musical analogy: the entire work is constructed like a cantata, with the young Christ as soloist. The two topmost angels are praying (figs. 55 and 56); the other ten play musical instruments, forming the chorus of this great lyric composition. Two by two, starting from the top (figs. 45 to 54), their red, blue, green or purple robes alternating against

figs. 41 to 43: **Predella of the Linaiuoli Triptych** 39 × 56 cm

a gold ground, they offer us the most delightful of concerts and complete the incredible impression of communication created by this work, as overwhelming in its inspiration as in its size.

When the wings are closed, the two majestic and gorgeously garbed saints make this tabernacle, commissioned by a secular body, an impressive religious work. The colorful movement of the predella panels offers a foretaste of the joy to be revealed once the wings are opened. The act of opening them will release in a very new way Fra Angelico's jubilant hymn of glorification and love of God.

Precious instant in a work infused with gravity, contemplation and awareness of the need to aspire to the Godhead, to transcend human suffering through the example of Christ the Savior.

fig. 44: **Detail from the Linaiuoli Triptych Virgin and Child Enthroned** (central panel)

fig. 45: Linaiuoli Triptych (detail)

figs. 46 to 56: **Linaiuoli Triptych** (details)

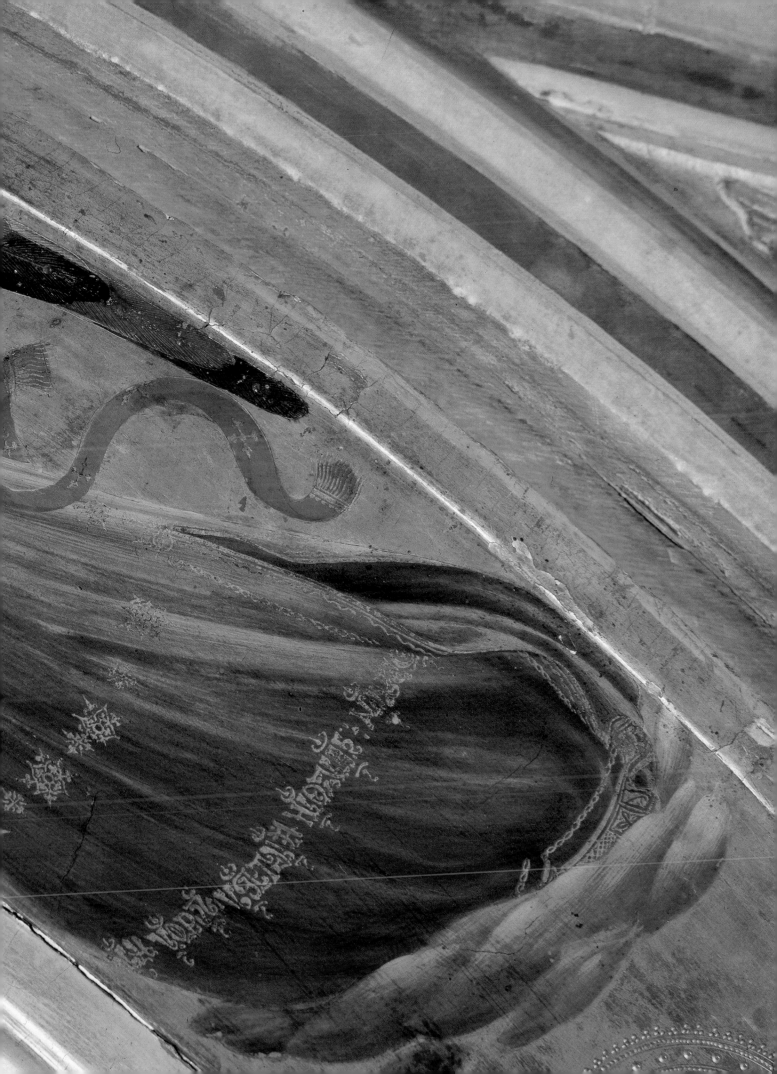

fig. 57: Lamentation over the Dead Christ (detail)

fig. 58: Lamentation over the Dead Christ, 1436
Panel painting 105 × 164 cm

On the horizontal bar of the T-shaped Cross
— how new it seems —
the nails bleed
from having bruised and torn
its smooth surface.

The ladder leads
nowhere.

The crenelated walls with countless
redoubts
gleam — the cold glint of metal —
lit sideways by a sun as pale as it is
invisible.

Hillocks
and bare slopes — mute and distant mountains
bristling with towers and frail castles.

The horizon
diffracts a gleam
of life that has ebbed away — the whole sky
echoes with it.

fig. 59: Lamentation over the Dead Christ (detail)

94

The huge door
gapes,
divulging the black suspicion of the city, compo-
    sed
of churches and towers.

No one
to come and see — to help? — at the scene
of the execution.

The trees of solitude
stand tall —
opposite the orange trees bearing golden
fruit; not one blade of grass
on this desolate heath.

The horizontal format of the *gisant* taken down
    from the cross has been
applied to other features in this painting:

The continuous line formed by the figures
facing us — a sorrowing Last Supper —
in attitudes of grief; the back of the woman
who bends to kiss the feet still suffering from the
    stigmata.

The endless
stretching of Christ's body,
floating barely supported,
resting on the upper part of the shoulders —
the face at rest, sublime — his purpose is ac-
    complished —
a weightless presence, as if in levitation.

A veil (an unsubstantial cloud?), not yet a
    shroud,
bears the body, abandoned
to the pain
the others feel.

The Virgin cradles
the heavy head.
The lips of the Son of Man will drink all
the Mother's tenderness.

The closed eyes are —
almost —
opened again
by a light from within.

Is this Death struggling
against the force that raises the still-flexible arms
from the stiffened chest?
Realism of
photographic quality.

The tones of yellow and gold —
heightened by ghostly white —
convey the pulse
of life — hope.

Is the end the beginning?

But man
cannot people
the wilderness by himself.
The fear that dwells in him
will be overcome
only by belief.

Beneath the cadaver of God
the grass and flowers
are reborn.

(following pages)

figs. 60 to 65: Details
from the Lamentation over the Dead Christ

96

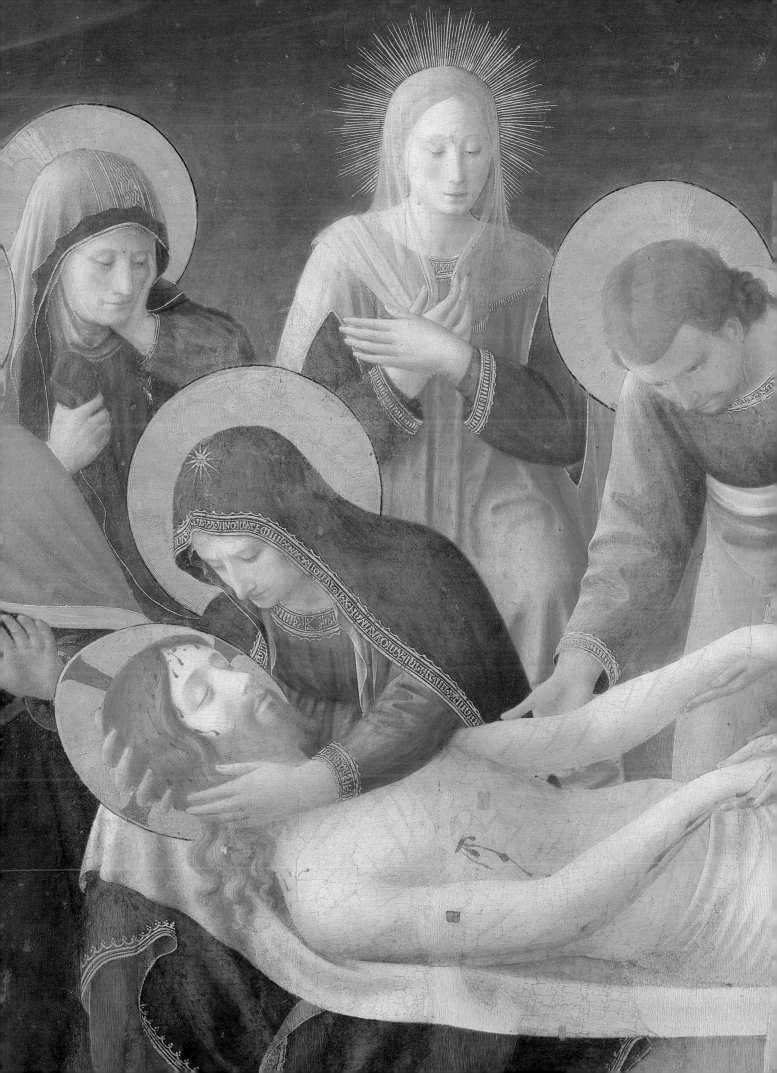

The green
of the saint's robe takes up the whole heart
of the painting — the many
reds
of the capes and robes
are powerless against it.

Dark bottomless
blue
is the color
of pain.

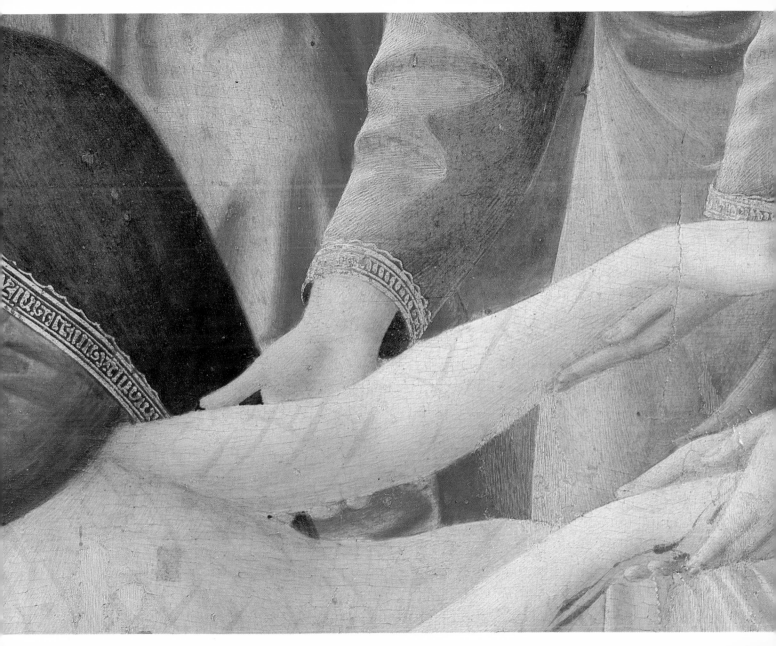

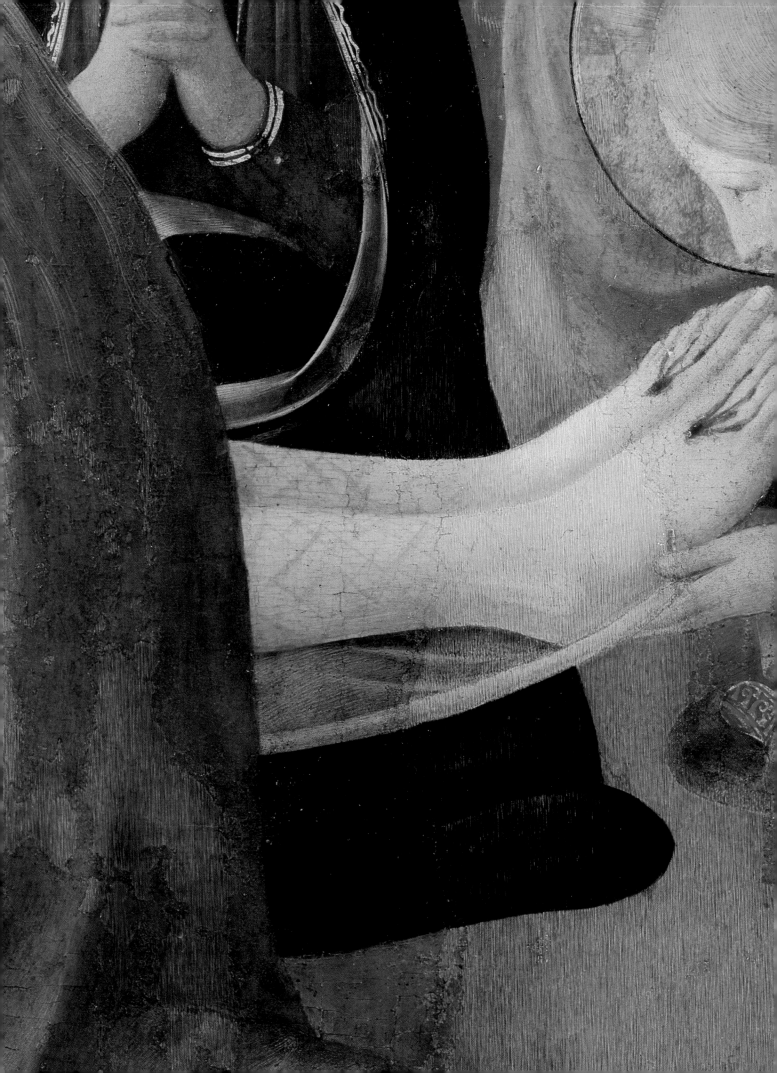

xpo ẏrv lamor mio crvcifisso

The San Marco Altarpiece*

Shall we wander very far away,
for a stroll in the Tuscan hills,
lying low on the horizon? Daylight
still prevails there,
for a while.

But already night
is covering the sky above us, its blueness
alive with the song of crickets. Joyously, gar-
    lands — festive lights? —
sway. Will those heavy
brocade curtains be closed
when the night grows cool?

But nature — our earthly body (do we possess
    nothing else?) —
is a watchful presence.
Massed together, the leafy trees and the ever-
    greens
of our chilly climates
scarcely tolerate the desert palm trees — tall
janissaries — twin lamps.
(Are their leaves not the symbol of
death for the faith?)

Abundance of
vegetable life, the secular life teeming,
procreating.

Should our spirits
find this troubling?

fig. 66: Detail from the Lamentation over the Dead Christ   * 1438-40 Panel painting 220 × 227 cm

107

A borderline
separates temporal reality from the seat of
  divinity,
which this altarpiece glorifies;
a length of light fabric has been carefully hung
on the inner side of the enclosure, at eye level;
the outside can take part in the life within.

Ah, the gravity of this encounter!
Jesus holds the world in his hand — and
  already
martyrdom, his destiny, transfigures him.

The angels with fluid, weighty
robes — two of them raise up the ornate veil on
  either side of the throne's plump cushions —
pay him discreet and respectful tribute.

(Look at the angel standing to the left of the
  Infant: did the young Piero della Francesca
  paint that face, in the days when he worked in
  Fra Giovanni's studio?)

It was in this work, dating from 1438-40, that Fra
  Angelico first put into practice the principles of perspective, codified in 1435 by Leo
  Battista Alberti in his treatise *De Pictura:*
  monumental figures in the foreground, the
  composition converging perfectly toward the
  rear in the symmetrical axis of the Brunel-
  leschian throne. The regular patterns of the
  Turkish rug measure off toward a vanishing
  point the prolonged space in which two saints
  are kneeling. St Cosmas turns to look at us.
  An unforgettable face!

Does Fra Giovanni, the militant friar, ever
  forget that his purpose in painting is to induce
  us to follow him higher and higher, to the
  loftiest peak of divinity?

Mounted in the larger painting, very close to
  us, is a golden tablet displaying a powerful
  Crucifixion (figs. 4 and 67). Its distinctly
  Gothic style is in strong contrast with the
  sumptuous texture of the altarpiece, a pinna-
  cle of the new art and evidence of the new
  philosophy paving the way for a new world.

Fra Angelico never entirely relinquished the Gothic style, not even when he and his contemporaries, the great creators and inquisitive minds of Florence, the Tuscan capital, produced their most stunning Renaissance

work. As always, the artist who breaks new ground does the most to protect his roots.

fig. 67: San Marco Altarpiece

Elsewhere we have discussed how gold was used as a color. Restorers, by weakening the chromatic values and damaging the painting to a disastrous extent with their outrageous use of paint removers, emphasized its "indoor scene" aspect at the expense of the distant landscape, which is almost obliterated. It is quite clear that in this painting Fra Angelico used the new technique of gold to the hilt. We need only look.

The two predella panels in the San Marco Museum — the seven other panels are in Washington, Munich and Paris — depict the burial of Saints Cosmas and Damian and the dream of the deacon Justinian, whose diseased leg the saints replaced with a healthy one taken from a dead Ethiopan.

The two small panels (37 × 45 cm) are indicative of Fra Angelico's new style. We have already seen, in connection with the predella of the Linaiuoli Triptych, how inventive he was in his use of such small formats. Here, we find not only a high degree of plastic beauty but an entirely new system of figuration obtained by the strict application of the laws of perspective.

The *Dream of the Deacon Justinian* (fig. 69) is a perfect example of this. Especially noteworthy is the way its strict and rigorous handling relates it to the frescoes (figs. 72 to 130) that Fra Angelico was to undertake, nearly one year later, in the cells of the convent of San Marco.

figs. 68, 69: **Predella of the San Marco Altarpiece**
Dream of the Deacon Justinian

The little scene is remarkably intimate and at the same time radiant, even sublime. Are we outside it, looking in? Or are we actually dreaming too?

The light gently caresses the hangings above the bed and throws a shadow onto the wall facing the small window. Through the opened door we glimpse other, lighted corridors.

What would happen if Justinian were to open his eyes and to see on the wall facing him — right here where we stand, watching him dream — a fresco painted by Fra Angelico?

The humble, everyday objects placed at the head of the bed and the stool near it tell us something about life in the convent. Yet we see no book, no table at which to work.

The overall tonal scheme is muted, subduing even the hyper-vivid reds.

The *Burial of Saints Cosmas and Damian* (fig. 70), on the contrary, is an outdoor scene. A priest reads the prayers for the dead; his acolytes stand on either side of the grave. Although the scene is supposed to take place in the Middle East, under Diocletian, the setting has a wholly Italian look. In fact, we can assume that it is Florence itself, and indeed the Piazza San Marco, in the middle of which a grave has been dug for the martyrs. The façades of the church and the convent form the background of the painting, and the street which leads off to the left could be the via Larga, one of the main streets of Florence.

The camel adds an exotic note, and its naturalism contrasts with the remarkably measured rhythm of the buildings. One very domestic detail is enough to convey the reality of urban living in the midst of this dramatic event: the earthenware flowerpot placed on the edge of the terrace, in the upper left corner (fig. 71).

In the shallow common grave, the haloed, decapitated martyrs have achieved beatitude. Will there be room for the fifth one, being dragged along on a shroud? The executioner-gravedigger, standing near us, on the right, seems to be pointing to an available space. These narrative details, in conjunction with the extensive use made of architectural lines and planes, have a contrapuntal effect.

So much familiarity, to achieve so much dignity! Who but Fra Angelico could have reached such heights of sacred harmony!

fig. 70: **Predella of the San Marco Altarpiece**
Burial of Saints Cosmas and Damian

fig. 71: **Detail from the Burial of Saints Cosmas and Damian**

And when the days of her purification according to the law of Moses were accomplished, they brought him to Jerusalem, to present him to the Lord; (As it is written in the law of the Lord, Every male that openeth the womb shall be called holy to the Lord;) And to offer a sacrifice according to that which is said in the law of the Lord, A pair of turtledoves, or two young pigeons. And, behold, there was a man in Jerusalem, whose name was Simeon; and the same man was just and devout, waiting for the consolation of Israel: and the Holy Ghost was upon him. And it was revealed unto him by the Holy Ghost, that he should not see death, before he had seen the Lord's Christ.

And he came by the Spirit into the temple: and when the parents brought in the child Jesus, to do for him after the custom of the law, Then took he him up in his arms, and blessed God, and said, Lord, now lettest thou thy servant depart in peace, according to thy word: For mine eyes have seen thy salvation, Which thou hast prepared before the face of all people; A light to lighten the Gentiles, and the glory of thy people Israel.

fig. 79. Detail from the Presentation in the Temple

135

The Presentation in the Temple

Fresco in cell 10

And when the days of her purification according to the law of Moses were accomplished, they brought him to Jerusalem, to present him to the Lord; (As it is written in the law of the Lord, Every male that openeth the womb shall be called holy to the Lord); And to offer a sacrifice according to that which is said in the law of the Lord, A pair of turtledoves, or two young pigeons. And, behold, there was a man in Jerusalem, whose name was Simeon; and the same man was just and devout, waiting for the consolation of Israel: and the Holy Ghost was upon him. And it was revealed unto him by the Holy Ghost, that he should not see death, before he had seen the Lord's Christ.

And he came by the Spirit into the temple: and when the parents brought in the child Jesus, to do for him after the custom of the law, Then took he him up in his arms, and blessed God, and said, Lord, now lettest thou thy servant depart in peace, according to thy word: For mine eyes have seen thy salvation, Which thou hast prepared before the face of all people; A light to lighten the Gentiles, and the glory of thy people Israel.

fig. 79: **Detail from the Presentation in the Temple**

And Joseph and his mother marvelled at those things which were spoken of him. And Simeon blessed them, and said unto Mary his mother, Behold, this child is set for the fall and rising again of many in Israel; and for a sign which shall be spoken against; (Yea, a sword shall pierce through thy own soul also,) that the thoughts of many hearts may be revealed.

And there was one Anna, a prophetess, the daughter of Phanuel, of the tribe of Aser: she was of a great age, and had lived with an husband seven years from her virginity; And she was a widow of about fourscore and four years, which departed not from the temple, but served God with fastings and prayers night and day.

And she coming in that instant gave thanks likewise unto the Lord, and spake of him to all them that looked for redemption in Jerusalem.

And when they had performed all things according to the law of the Lord, they returned into Galilee, to their own city Nazareth.

links the basket of doves
to the Infant King.

The sacrificial fire burns on the altar,
which is magnified by the radiating lines of the
niche.
God watches over and illuminates
the encounter.
The Child who inspires the old man
to prophesy
appears to have a mischievous grasp
of wisdom and knowledge.

figs. 80 to 85 Detail from the Presentation in the Temple

And Joseph and his mother marvelled at those things which were spoken of him. And Simeon blessed them, and said unto Mary his mother, Behold, this child is set for the fall and rising again of many in Israel; and for a sign which shall be spoken against; (Yea, a sword shall pierce through thy own soul also), that the thoughts of many hearts may be revealed.

And there was one Anna, a prophetess, the daughter of Phanuel, of the tribe of Aser: she was of a great age, and had lived with an husband seven years from her virginity; And she was a widow of about fourscore and four years, which departed not from the temple, but served God with fastings and prayers night and day.

And she, coming in that instant, gave thanks likewise unto the Lord, and spake of him to all them that looked for redemption in Jerusalem.

And when they had performed all things according to the law of the Lord, they returned into Galilee, to their own city Nazareth.

Luke 2, 22-39

One line —
an aisle of hands —
links the basket of doves
to the Infant King.

The sacrificial fire burns on the altar,
which is magnified by the radiating lines of the
    niche.
God watches over and illuminates
the encounter.
The Child who inspires the old man
to prophesy
appears to have a mischievous grasp
of wisdom and knowledge.

figs. 80 to 83: **Details from the Presentation in the Temple**

His gaze — the two eyes transparent with
    certainty —
transfixes Simeon,
stunned
by relevation.

The bodies
are vibrant beneath the drapery of their
    garments —
compact vertical masses of iridescent colors —
torches
whose flames are the haloed
faces.

They float,
suspended above the podium,
ranged tight within the picture plane,
horizontality emphasizing
oneness.

Peter Martyr and Beata Villana
in the foreground
bring to us, as spectators
in the shadows,
a glimmer of participation.

The silence of the cell,
violated day and night
by the violent inburst
of the Florentine sky,
provides the setting for what may be
Angelico's purest manner.

Revelation of faith —
simplicity itself —
and each man re-creates
his own communication with the infinitude
of God.

fig. 84: **Presentation in the Temple**, 1440-1
Fresco 158 × 136 cm. Cell 10

His gaze — the two eyes transparent with
certainty —
transfixes Simeon,
stunned
by relevation.

The bodies
are vibrant beneath the drapery of their
garments —
compact vertical masses of iridescent colors —
torches
whose flames are the haloed
faces.

They float,
suspended above the podium,
ranged tight within the picture plane,
horizontality emphasizing
oneness.

Peter Martyr and Beata Villana
in the foreground
bring to us, as spectators
in the shadows,
a glimmer of participation.

The silence of the cell,
violated day and night
by the violent inburst
of the Florentine sky,
provides the setting for what may be
Angelico's purest manner.

Revelation of faith —
simplicity itself —
and each man re-creates
his own communication with the infinitude
of God.

fig. 84: Presentation in the Temple, 1440-
Fresco 158 × 286 cm. Cell 10

An ocean of white
The oppressor's cloth
binds Christ's eyes — a shroud before the

The multitude
of blows gestures powerless to destroy
the derisiveness
of spittle in his face.

He accepts.

Not a cry
the victim is bereft of everything
before the determination of his torturers.

These moments are unbearable
Mary and Dominic
refuse to watch.

The spitter dares him — sterile taunt —
"Prophesy!"
But Jesus Christ needs no crystal ball.
In his hands
the evil staff forcing down the dolorous
crown —
athwart and unsupported;

The hand that strikes, floats in space:
the one preparing to strike
appears
to query.

Bright red
the clearly outlined mouth,
fleshy, sensual,
keeping silent.

Unsullied
Truth.

And the men that held Jesus mocked him, and smote him. And when they had blindfolded him, they struck him on the face, and asked him, saying, Prophesy, who is it that smote thee?

And many other things blasphemously spake they against him.

The Mocking of Christ

Fresco in cell 7

And the men that held Jesus mocked him, and smote him, And when they had blindfolded him, they struck him on the face, and asked him, saying, Prophesy, who is it that smote thee?

And many other things blasphemously spake they against him.

Luke 22, 63-65

An ocean of white
sheds light on our dazzled gaze.
The oppressor's cloth
binds Christ's eyes — a shroud before the
  Shroud —
Torture hounds the invincible.

The multitude
of blows, gestures powerless to destroy;
the derisiveness
of spittle in his face.

He accepts.

Not a cry,
the victim is bereft of everything
before the determination of his torturers.

These moments are unbearable.
Mary and Dominic
refuse to watch.

The spitter dares him — sterile taunt! —
"Prophesy!"
But Jesus Christ needs no crystal ball.
In his hands
he holds the emblems of royalty.

Staff for staff:
the staff of peace firmly upright;
the evil staff forcing down the dolorous
  crown —
athwart and unsupported.

The hand that strikes, floats in space;
the one preparing to strike
appears
to query.

Bright red
the clearly outlined mouth,
fleshly, sensual,
keeping silent.

Unsullied
Truth.

fig. 85: Mocking of Christ, 1440-1
Fresco 188 × 164 cm. Cell 7

figs. 86 to 90: Details from the Mocking of Christ

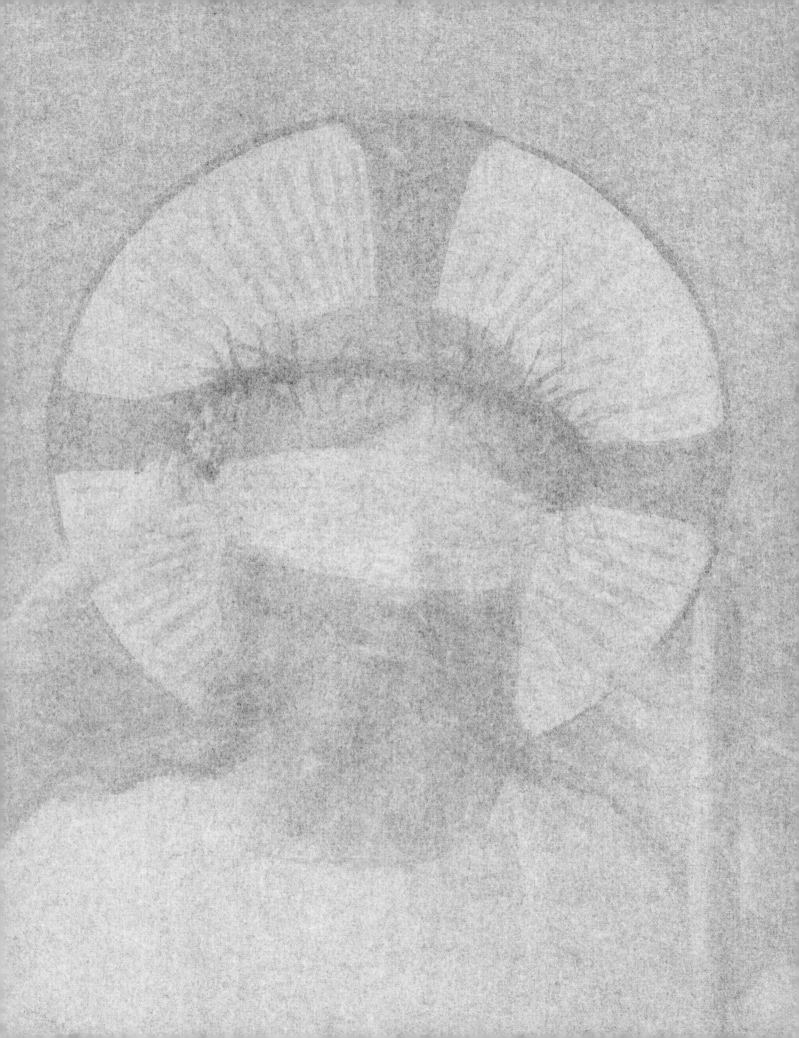

The Coronation of the Virgin

Fresco in cell 9

The cult of Mary has grown steadily within the Catholic church. Although the Gospels accord the Mother of God-made-man only scant recognition of her divine nature, devotion to Mary eventually assumed a place of privilege in the hearts of the faithful and in religious practice.

The Coronation of the Virgin by her Son is a scene frequently encountered in religious iconography, and the greatest artists have chosen to depict it.

Fra Angelico here sets off the spiritual world of the divine against the temporal world of religion.

The pictorial treatment of the figures endows the Virgin and Christ with an other-worldliness accentuated by the realism of the saints — Thomas, Benedict, Dominic, Francis — Peter Martyr and Mark — a Who's Who of the blessed. Their robes are drawn with methodical precision; their halos weigh upon their shoulders, as the cord tied about St. Francis's waist rests upon the ground.

The semicircular arrangement in the foreground is no mere decorative, unconvincing garland, for its function is to situate the subject: a coterie of saints for a divine liturgy.

Haloed by a moonlight glow as incandescent as the sun,
Mother and Son are seated.
A mass of clouds —
like horizontal moldings —
provides support for the bodies, well-structured yet so immaterial
in their immaculate raiment.

Other clouds beneath their feet absorb the spread-out folds of drapery;
this blending symbolizes the all-pervading spirit of Mother and Son.

Their very presence is distilled in their faces and their hands — the deference of prayer, the gesture of crowning.

The upper portions of their bodies come together in the golden tiara, studded with pearls and precious stones, situated at the highest point of the fresco's axis. And then we realize that all these circles — accentuated by the white shape behind them, the original nimbus (God the Father) — obey another imperative, that of the triangle governing Creation — the Holy Trinity — whose apex in this painting is the tiara placed by God (love and meditation) upon the Mother's head. A strong and noble gesture, expressive of the greatest tenderness.

We are carried away by emotion and even more by Fra Angelico's mastery, for the way he arranges the masses of light tones and the darker areas is a fine example of his art of composition — his sensitive architecture of forms and colors directs the dynamics of contrasts in such a way that his subject is handled with the greatest economy and the most perfect clarity.

He plays on verticality — and also on our memory, which links here the sacred moments of the Ascension and the Assumption — by creating over the heads of the men of Prayer a physical, above all a mental, zone of dazzlement, resuming his narration at the summit of the composition, accuracy of line and color contributing to an ascending movement, as warm air lifts a balloon, drawing human aspiration toward the Absolute.

figs. 92 to 94: Details from the Coronation of the Virgin

The Coronation of the Virgin

Fresco in cell 9

The cult of Mary has grown steadily within the Catholic church. Although the Gospels accord the Mother of God-made-man only scant recognition of her divine nature, devotion to Mary eventually assumed a place of privilege in the hearts of the faithful and in religious practice.

The Coronation of the Virgin by her Son is a scene frequently encountered in religious iconography, and the greatest artists have chosen to depict it.

Fra Angelico here sets off the spiritual world of the divine against the temporal world of religion.

The pictorial treatment of the figures endows the Virgin and Christ with an other-worldliness accentuated by the realism of the saints — Thomas, Benedict, Dominic, Francis, Peter Martyr and Mark — a Who's Who of the blessed. Their robes are drawn with methodical precision; their halos weigh upon their shoulders, as the cord tied about St. Francis's waist rests upon the ground.

The semicircular arrangement in the foreground is no mere decorative, unconvincing garland, for its function is to situate the subject: a Cantoria of saints for a divine liturgy.

Haloed by a moonlight glow as incandescent as
  the sun,
Mother and Son are seated.
A mass of clouds —
like horizontal moldings —
provides support for the bodies, well-structured
yet so immaterial
in their immaculate raiment.

Other clouds beneath their feet absorb the
  spread-out folds of drapery;
this blending symbolizes the all-pervading
spirit of Mother and Son.

Their very presence is distilled in their faces and their hands — the deference of prayer, the gesture of crowning.

The upper portions of their bodies come together in the golden tiara, studded with pearls and precious stones, situated at the highest point of the fresco's axis. And then we realize that all these circles — accentuated by the white shape behind them, the original nebula (God the Father?) — obey another imperative, that of the triangle governing Creation — the Holy Trinity — whose apex in this painting is the tiara placed by God (love and meditation) upon the Mother's head. A strong and noble gesture, expressive of the greatest tenderness.

We are carried away by emotion and even more by Fra Angelico's mastery, for the way he arranges the masses of light tones and the darker areas is a fine example of his art of composition — his sensitive architecture of forms and colors directs the dynamics of contrasts in such a way that his subject is handled with the greatest economy and the most perfect clarity.

He plays on verticality — and also on our
  memory, which links here the sacred moments
  of the Ascension and the Assumption —
by creating over the heads of the men of Prayer
a physical,
above all a mental, zone of dazzlement;
resuming his narration at the summit of the
  composition,
accuracy of line and color contributing
to an ascending movement, as warm air lifts a
  balloon, drawing human
aspiration toward the Absolute.

fig. 91: Coronation of the Virgin, 1440-1
Fresco 184 × 167 cm. Cell 9

figs. 92 to 95: Details from the Coronation of the Virgin

God had dwelt the space
in which the prophets float
Elias and Moses — their words
silence this moment unlike any other.

The Word and the Spirit become flesh
for these human beings
who have nothing but their faith
and their astonishment.

O work,
the Virgin and Dominic
accept this extraordinary event.

"This
is my beloved Son,
In whom
I am well pleased."

Here in cell 6,
more than anywhere else,
the painter worked in a state of grace.
His narrative means are amplified in the extreme:
amplicity of a tale reduced to its minimum,
reduced even to naivete.

An inner breath magnifies the whole.
The use of white —
not the fact, but the idea of absolute white —
transfigures all.

Oval
of the cloud —
semblance of the fleshly
body
triumph on the rock?
The tangible world
burning
with a flame made of music.

Richly scored polyphony
of bodies and faces
to encounter the great Voice
of the Divine.

We who know how this Man's story ended —
where Redemption began —
will seek in vain upon these hands,
so wide open to our cruelty,
the stigmata of his ordeal.

God the Body — Christ
God the Holy Spirit — Cloud
God the Father — Voice

Cloud billowing above the horizon.
Jesus grows enormously tall.
His arms
stretched wide
embrace
the whole universe.

The Voice resounds
amid the radiating light.
Thunderous, the affrighted gestures
panic
of John, James and Peter.

The power
in the Man's eyes.

fig. 90 Transfiguration, 1440-1
Fresco in San Marco, Cell 6
fig. 91-98 Details from the Transfiguration

The Transfiguration

Fresco in cell 6

God the Body — Christ
God the Holy Spirit — Cloud
God the Father — Voice.

Cloud billowing above the horizon,
Jesus grows enormously tall.
His arms
stretched wide
embrace
the whole universe.

The Voice resounds
amid the radiating light,
thunderous din, affrighted gestures,
panic
of John, James and Peter.

The power
in the Man's eyes.

Godhead swells the space
in which the prophets float:
Elias and Moses — their words
sanction this moment unlike any other.

The Word and the Spirit become flesh
for these human beings
who have nothing but their faith
and their astonishment.

Gravely,
the Virgin and Dominic
accept this extraordinary event.

"This
is my beloved Son,
in whom
I am well pleased."

Here in cell 6,
more than anywhere else,
the painter worked in a state of grace.
His narrative means are simplified in the
    extreme:
simplicity of a tale reduced to its minimum,
reduced even to naïveté.

An inner breath magnifies the whole.
The use of white —
not the fact but the idea of absolute white —
transfigures all.

Oval
of the cloud —
or radiance of the fleshly
body,
upright on the rock?
The tangible world
burning
with a flame made of music.

Richly scored polyphony
of bodies and faces
to encounter the great Voice
of the Divine.

We who know how this Man's story ended —
where Redemption began —
will seek in vain upon these hands,
so wide open to our scrutiny,
the stigmata of his ordeal.

fig. 96: Transfiguration, 1440-1
Fresco 193 × 164 cm. Cell 6
figs. 97, 98: Details from the Transfiguration

The "Behold the handmaid of the Lord —"
spoken by she who receives
— the gift of God —
has just been uttered.

The light comes from high up
under the vaulted ceiling
that shades
the peristyle,
and gently graces the virgin woman.

The angel Gabriel is about to bow
and resume his flight.
His message still within him,
the intensity of his gaze
reveals
the warmth
and importance
of his mission.

left, see to text: Details from the Annunciation

The "Behold the handmaid of the Lord" —
spoken by she who receives
the gift of God —
has just been uttered.

The light comes from high up
under the vaulted ceiling
that shades
the peristyle,
and gently graces the virgin woman.

The angel Gabriel is about to bow
and resume his flight.
His message still within him,
the intensity of his gaze
reveals
the warmth
and importance
of his mission.

figs. 100 to 102: Details from the Annunciation

Vibrant pulsations —
plenitude of this moment —
revolving within the narrow space
in which the future of the world
is announced.

The spirit grants life and fills the space entirely.

The profiles
answer one another —
osmosis at its utmost
like
the issue of essence and essence.
The fiery glow
of the angel's hair
balances the pure glow
of the maiden's forehead. All
is rounded, revolving
imperceptibly
upon itself.

There are angles too: those of the soft wood
stool elevating the Annunciate;
those
of the open book —
an instinctive gesture protects it;
the page is still
virgin.

Intimacy to be revealed,
in which the Holy Martyr participates from
without.
Everyone
can take part.
The truth
must burst forth! — and
through the little door at the back,
even we
can enter into it.

Vibrant pulsations —
plenitude of this moment —
revolving within the narrow space
in which the future of the world
is announced.

The spirit grants life and fills the space entirely.

The profiles
answer one another —
osmosis at its utmost —
like
the issue of essence and essence.
The fiery glow
of the angel's hair
balances the pure glow
of the maiden's forehead. All
is rounded, revolving
imperceptibly
upon itself.

There are angles too: those of the soft wood
    stool elevating the Annunciate;
those
of the open book —
an instinctive gesture protects it;
the page is still
virgin.

Intimacy to be revealed,
in which the Holy Martyr participates from
    without.
Everyone
can take part.
The truth
must burst forth! — and
through the little door at the back,
even we
can enter into it.

figs. 103 to 105: Details from the Annunciation

VIRGINIS INTACTE CVM VENERIS ANTE FIGVRAM PRETEREVNDO CAVE NE SILEATVR AVE

The outer world is a gaping
presence,
despite the enclosure and the trees
shutting off the distance.

It invades the
wide-open room, in a triangular
thrust
whose apex reaches the womb
of the seated Virgin.

The arrested movement of the angel, knee bent
and torso leaning forward,
accentuates the tension.

Here
the faces differ. The angel's
face is sharp,
youthful and ambiguous.
The Virgin, whose exquisitely drawn features
had never been expressed so purely, is
gravity itself.

It is as if the artist's maturity had taken over
his subject, and his palette too —
almost ponderous
in its warmth.

That little barred window
in the background:
Does it disturb the harmony?
like a danger warded off.

In this fresco, the event
is so momentous, so suspended in time,
that it seems
far less happy.

fig. 109: Annunciation (detail)

The outer world is a gaping
presence,
despite the enclosure and the trees
shutting off the distance.

It invades the
wide-open room, in a triangular
thrust
whose apex reaches the womb
of the seated Virgin.

The arrested movement of the angel, knee bent
and torso leaning forward,
accentuates the tension.

Here
the faces differ. The angel's
face is sharp,
youthful and ambiguous.
The Virgin, whose exquisitely drawn features
had never been expressed so purely, is
gravity itself.

It is as if the artist's maturity had taken over
his subject, and his palette too —
almost ponderous
in its warmth.

That little barred window
in the background:
Does it disturb the harmony?
like a danger warded off.

that it seems
far less happy

The large Crucifixion*
Sala del Capitolo

Now there stood by the cross of Jesus his mother, and his mother's sister, Mary the wife of Cleophas, and Mary Magdalene. When Jesus therefore saw his mother, and the disciple standing by, whom he loved, he saith unto his mother, Woman, behold thy son! Then saith he to the disciple, Behold thy mother! And from that hour that disciple took her unto his own home.

After this, Jesus knowing that all things were now accomplished, that the scripture might be fulfilled, saith, I thirst. Now there was set a vessel full of vinegar: and they filled a sponge with vinegar, and put it upon hyssop, and put it to his mouth. When Jesus therefore had received the vinegar, he said, It is finished: and he bowed his head, and gave up the ghost.

The Jews therefore, because it was the preparation, that the bodies should not remain upon the cross on the sabbath day, (for that sabbath day was an high day,) besought Pilate that their legs might be broken, and that they might be taken away.

Then came the soldiers, and brake the legs of the first, and of the other which was crucified with him. But when they came to Jesus, and saw that he was dead already, they brake not his legs: But one of the soldiers with a spear pierced his side, and forthwith came there out blood and water.

And he that saw it bare record, and his record is true: and he knoweth that he saith true, that ye might believe. For these things were done, that the scripture should be fulfilled, A bone of him shall not be broken. And again another scripture saith, They shall look on him whom they pierced.

John 19, 25-37

* 1441-2 Fresco   550 × 950 cm.

figs. 110 to 112: Details from the Crucifixion with Attendant Saints

This large fresco, nearly 33 feet long, is in the Sala del Capitolo, on the ground floor of the convent; it covers the wall facing the door that leads to the cloister.

The fresco is over 16 feet high at its central axis, where Fra Angelico has placed the cross of Christ. The artist has created a powerful perspective effect by situating in the background behind this the crosses of the two thieves.

Jesus, shown life-size, appears to be thrust forward, in his solitude, seems more present, more monumental than ever. He towers above us; the fresco begins at a certain height above the floor, suggesting that we as spectators are standing at the foot of the knoll where the execution is taking place.

The foreground, with its twenty sorrowing figures, could well situate the scene in the present. Yet the shock we feel does not come from the story. What we see here is not so much the realistic recital of the death of Christ as a collective reflection on its significance: the willing Sacrifice of God-made-man.

Thus, Fra Angelico achieved his objective in carrying out this commission for Cosimo de' Medici: to enshrine for permanent contemplation by the friars the moment of God the Savior's suffering. The figures fall into groups formed by their attitudes, less expressive of the nature of communication than is the overall rhythm of the painting, which is conveyed by the placement of the masses and the number and variety of the colors.

It is our good fortune that this fresco was recently restored, for the restoration has almost succeeded in reinstating the original values of the composition. The three crosses had come to stand out harshly against a flat, abstract sky, overdramatized by the blue of the lapis lazuli. The red that until recently appeared to be the background color was actually the red of the primer coat; it had been intended to contrast with, and therefore reinforce, the intense blue of the powdered lapis but had gradually overtaken the entire background.

Enough of the original blue has been reconstituted to give us a more sensitive feeling of this fresco.

A frieze of figures surrounds the composition. Those below — sixteen saints and beatifieds, ranged on either side of St. Dominic in the center — are entwined in the sinuous curves of a branch. Above are nine patriarchs, brandishing inscriptions. In the center, above the cross, is a pelican (symbolizing Redemption). In the right-hand corner is the Erythraean Sybil, perhaps proclaiming her oracle.

The plastic quality of the crucified bodies prefigures that of others, such as those of the two thieves as drawn by Lucas Cranach the Elder (Dahlem Museum, Berlin).

The Virgin, about to swoon with sorrow, is held erect by the Holy Women; we are struck by this intimate glimpse of her grief, caught as if by a snapshot. Each group is similarly raptured, in its own moment of suspended time.

Although it has been said of this large Crucifixion that many of Fra Angelico's pupils worked on it, we are struck by its total impact, as grandiose as a funeral symphony.

Conceived by Fra Angelico for the purpose of confirming us more consciously in our faith, it moves us, as overwhelming as the unexpected sight of megaliths amid the vast sweep of a deserted heath.

figs. 213 to 231 Details from the Crucifixion with Attendant Saints

This large fresco, nearly 33 feet long, is in the *Sala del Capitolo*, on the ground floor of the convent; it covers the wall facing the door that leads to the cloister.

The fresco is over 16 feet high at its central axis, where Fra Angelico has placed the cross of Christ. The artist has created a powerful perspective effect by situating in the background behind this the crosses of the two thieves.

Jesus, shown life-size, appears to be thrust, forward and, in his solitude, seems more present, more monumental than ever. He towers above us; the fresco begins at a certain height above the floor, suggesting that we as spectators are standing at the foot of the knoll where the execution is taking place.

The foreground, with its twenty sorrowing figures, could well situate the scene in the present. Yet the shock we feel does not come from the story. What we see here is not so much the realistic recital of the death of Christ as a collective reflection on its significance: the willing *Sacrifice* of God-made-man.

Thus, Fra Angelico achieved his objective in carrying out this commission for Cosimo de' Medici: to enshrine for permanent contemplation by the friars the moment of God the Savior's suffering. The figures fall into groups formed by their attitudes, less expressive of the nature of communication than is the overall rhythm of the painting, which is conveyed by the placement of the masses and the number and variety of the colors.

It is our good fortune that this fresco was recently restored, for the restoration has almost succeeded in reinstating the original values of the composition. The three crosses had come to stand out harshly against a flat, abstract sky, overdramatized by the blue of the lapis lazuli. The red that until recently appeared to be the background color was actually the red of the primer coat; it had been intended to contrast with, and therefore reinforce, the intense blue of the powdered lapis but had gradually overtaken the entire background.

Enough of the original blue has been reconstituted to give us a more sensitive feeling of this fresco.

A frieze of figures surrounds the composition. Those below — sixteen saints and beatifieds, ranged on either side of St. Dominic in the center — are entwined in the sinuous curves of a branch. Above are nine patriarchs, brandishing inscriptions. In the center, above the cross, is a pelican (symbolizing Redemption). In the right-hand corner is the Erythrean Sybil, perhaps proclaiming her oracle.

The plastic quality of the crucified bodies prefigures that of others, such as those of the two thieves as drawn by Lucas Cranach the Elder (Dahlem Museum, Berlin).

The Virgin, about to swoon with sorrow, is held erect by the Holy Women; we are struck by this intimate glimpse of her grief, caught as if by a snapshot. Each group is similarly captured, in its own moment of suspended time.

Although it has been said of this large *Crucifixion* that many of Fra Angelico's pupils worked on it, we are struck by its total impact, as grandiose as a funeral symphony.

Conceived by Fra Angelico for the purpose of confirming us more consciously in our faith, it moves us, as overwhelming as the unexpected sight of megaliths amid the vast sweep of a deserted heath.

figs. 113 to 117: **Details from the Crucifixion with Attendant Saints**

SIMILIS FACTV VM PELLICANO SOLITVDINIS

יהושע צא צר כלרה יהורים
ΙΟΟ ΝΑΖ ΩΡΑΙΟΟ ΒΑCΙΛΕΥCΤΩΝΙΟΑΛΙΩΝ
IESVS NAZARENVS REX IVDEORVM

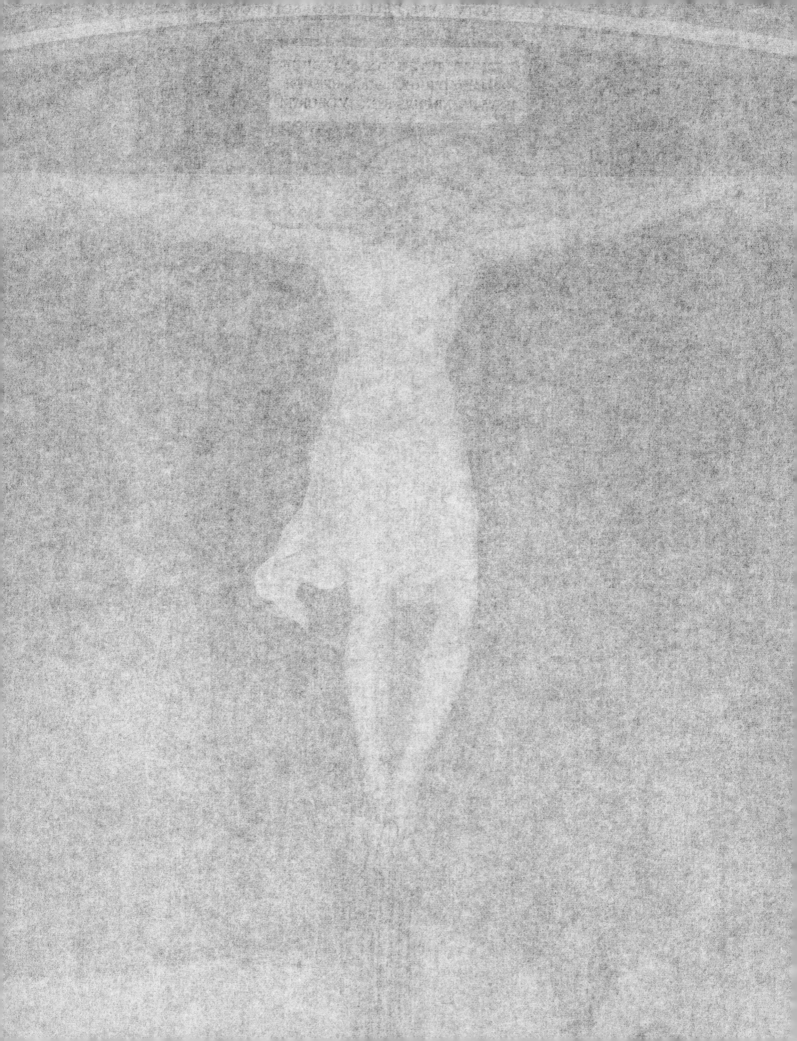

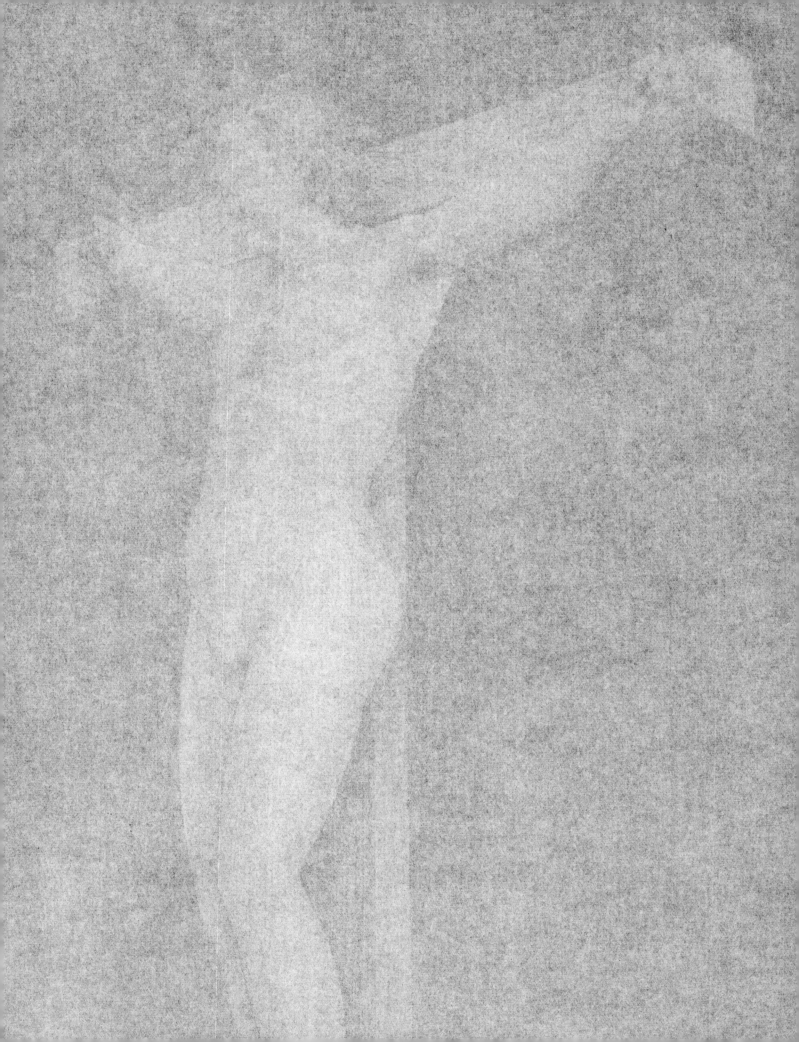

Christ on the Cross Adored by St Dominic

Cloister

Red coagulates on the lips
of the wound,
pierced by the soldier's lance,
it oozes water and blood.
The hard black nails no longer constrain
the flesh —
it bleeds abundantly.

The storm's last breath
twists the loincloth. The
empty sky arches over
the night-dark horizon
of Golgotha.

Dominic, alone,
absorbs the great silence.
Have they all deserted?

His neck is stiff
with the effort to support
the dead man.
But the cross
is not the body — the wood streams
with blood, so close to him.

Will the gift of his faith
be made one
with the Redeemer's
gift of life?

Though this be impossible,
it must always be attempted.

Unflagging
determination
to become one
with him who suffers,
to accept the ascetic's life,

fig. 118. Crucifixion with Attendant Saints, 1441-2.
Fresco 550 × 950 cm. Sala del Capitolo

figs. 119, 121, 122. Details from the Christ on the Cross
Adored by St Dominic

Christ on the Cross Adored by St Dominic

Cloister

Red coagulates on the lips
of the wound;
pierced by the soldier's lance,
it oozes water and blood.
The hard black nails no longer constrain
the flesh —
it bleeds abundantly.

The storm's last breath
twists the loincloth. The
empty sky arches over
the night-dark horizon
of Golgotha.

Dominic, alone,
absorbs the great silence.
Have they all deserted?

His neck is stiff
with the effort to support
the dead man.
But the cross
is not the body — the wood streams
with blood, so close to him.

Will the gift of his faith
be made one
with the Redeemer's
gift of life?

Though this be impossible,
it must always be attempted.

Unflagging
determination
to become one
with him who suffers,
to accept the ascetic's life.

fig. 118: Crucifixion with Attendant Saints, 1441-2
Fresco 550 × 950 cm. Sala del Capitolo

figs. 119, 121, 122: Details from the Christ on the Cross
Adored by St Dominic

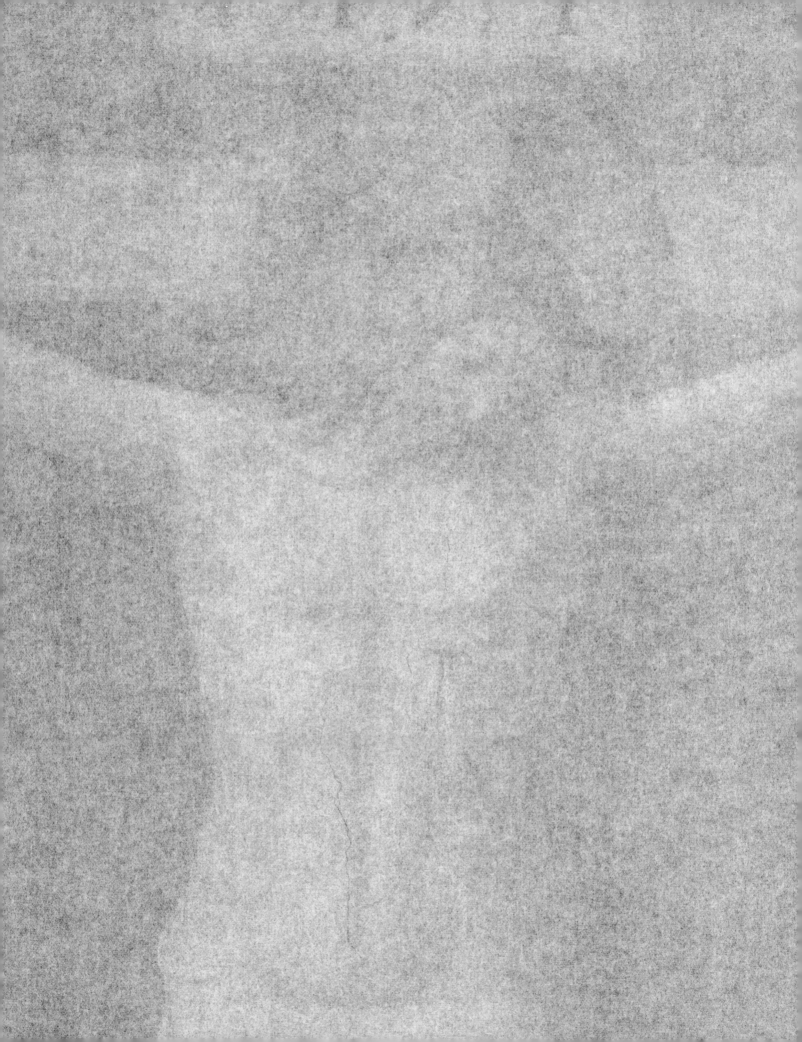

This is the source of all San Marco's sublime
imagery.
It is not surprising
that Fra Angelico produced what is without a
doubt
this miracle of faith
here,
after all the others.

Quietude
and repose — the Divine Purpose has been
accomplished.
Elder brother to the Jesus in the Deposition of
Santa Trinita,
the least stereotyped
of all the Christs ever depicted.
Never since have they been painted thus, with
photographic realism.

The entrance to the convent leads us straight
to this very large composition. Not even the
cedar
in the cloister garden
can distract us

This is the source of all San Marco's sublime
    imagery.
It is not surprising
that Fra Angelico produced what is without a
    doubt
this miracle of faith
here,
after all the others.

Quietude
and repose — the Divine Purpose has been
    accomplished.
Ah, this face! the truest possible.
Is it a portrait?
Elder brother to the Jesus in the *Deposition* of
    Santa Trinita,
the least stereotyped
of all the Christs ever depicted.
Never since have they been painted thus, with
    photographic realism.

The entrance to the convent leads us straight
to this very large composition. Not even the
    cedar
in the cloister garden
can distract us
from it.

fig. 120: **Christ on the Cross Adored by
St Dominic**, c. 1442 . Fresco 340 × 155 cm

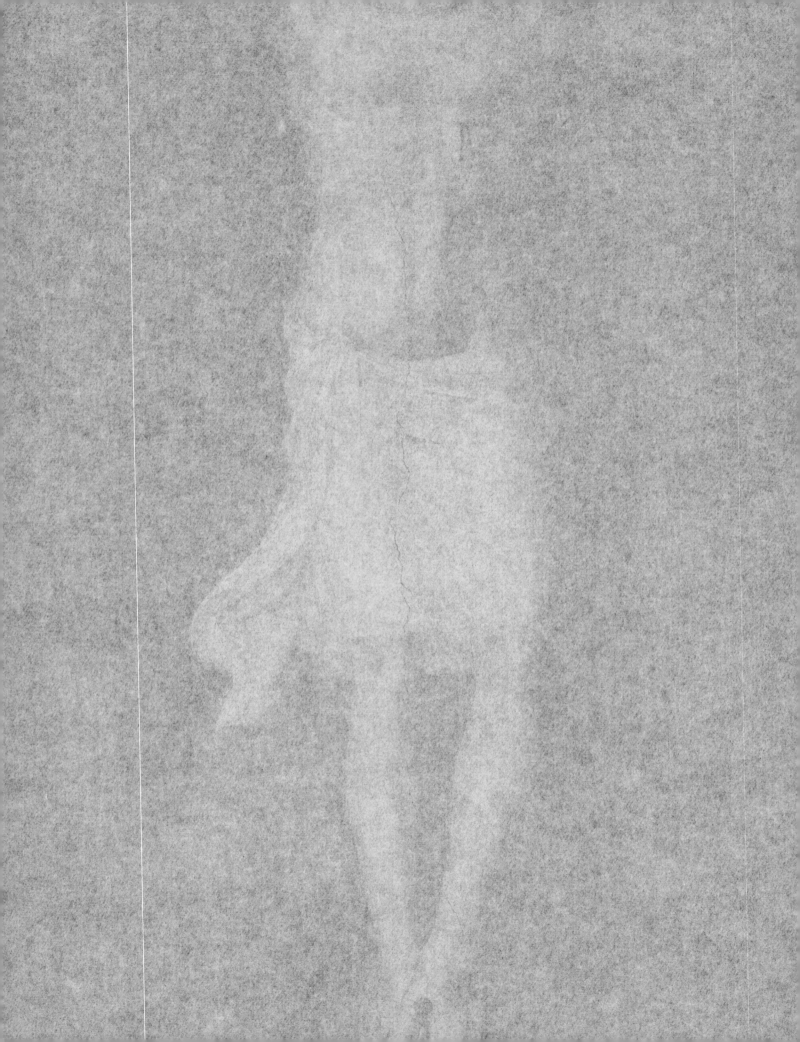

The Virgin and Child Enthroned with Eight Saints

How surprising is this noble — and already classic — composition! It is on the inner wall of the east corridor on the second floor. Does the visitor have enough curiosity to contemplate this painting — placed in transit as it were in this lateral space — as it deserves?

The visitor has just felt the impact of the great *Annunciation,* at the head of the stairs leading to the upper floor. Immediately afterward he has entered the first cells, the ones in which Fra Giovanni, artist and man of faith, distilled the most highly charged and powerful aspects of his art so as to create, with the barest of means, active places of meditation. From these paintings, the Dominican friars, in their aspiration toward God, could draw the strength necessary for the elevation of their souls.

A large number of the frescoes shown in this volume must be sought in these separate cells (which is why it is so difficult to grasp Fra Angelico's pictorial achievement in its entirety): *Noli Me Tangere* (cell 1), the *Annunciation* (cell 3), the *Transfiguration* (cell 6), the *Mocking of Christ* (cell 7), the *Coronation of the Virgin* (cell 9), the *Presentation in the Temple* (cell 10) — not to mention many other cells in which Fra Angelico's pupils and disciples carried out, often with supreme skill, works forming part of the master's grand design.

But even given these circumstances, neither the location of the painting nor the emotions the visitor has already felt by the time he reaches it explain why it has received so little attention.

Fra Angelico painted it for the convent, a world cut off from the world, each of whose members had his whole life in which to meditate on it. For a friar, the encounter with such a composition at this particular place in the gallery was a premeditated act. Did the painter intend to create, at this precise point, a different kind of link — a greater awareness of the world? a closer tie to the times?

If in fact there is anything surprising about this work, it is the style itself. When was it painted? Everything points to a date after Fra Angelico's return from Rome: the architecture of the setting, of which the Virgin's throne is part; the modeling of the faces (which, as is often the case with the paintings on wood panel, prefigure those of Piero della Francesca); the patterns decorating the garments and the fabric draped over the throne; the ample blue mass of the Virgin's robes, providing stability at the center of a space which might otherwise appear too vast. The two groups of saints — on the right, John the Evangelist, Thomas Aquinas, Lawrence (with his gridiron), and Peter Martyr; on the left, Mark, Damian, Cosmas and Dominic — form a guard of honor which leaves much of the foreground empty, inviting the viewer's eyes to go straight to the divine group of Mother and Child, to penetrate to the heart of the scene.

It has been suggested that Fra Angelico's assistants worked on this fresco. Indeed that is probable, considering the practices common at the time, and more specifically during this period of the artist's career following the frescoes he painted in Rome and Orvieto — provided we agree, that is, to date the work sometime after 1447-49. In this, as in general throughout the present study, we accept Sir John Pope-Hennessy's dating, based on the relationship of the fresco with the Bosco ai Frati Altarpiece, now in the San Marco Museum (see below, figs. 153 to 160), which was painted between 1450 and 1452.

figs. 123 to 125, 127 to 130: Details from the Virgin and Child Enthroned with Eight Saints

fig. 126: Virgin and Child Enthroned with Eight Saints c. 1450
Fresco 205 × 273 cm. West corridor

CARITATEM
HĒTE. HVM
ILITATEM
SERVATE.
PAVPERT
ATEM VO
LVNTARI

AM POSSI
DETE. MALE
DICTOÑE DEI 7
MEA ĪPRECOR
POSSESSIONES
Ī DVCĒTI THŌ
ORDINE.

SBM MCM
ITIVM EV
NGELII VHV
SIC SCP
E TISAYA
A. ECCE E
MICTO A
LVM MEV

AN FACIE
TVA QVI
TABIT V
IAM TVA
EN TE.VOX
CLAMATIS
DESTO P

Executed for the *Strozzi* chapel of the sacristy in the church of *Santa Trinita*, this work reveals new developments in *Fra Giovanni's* art.

Lorenzo Monaco had begun to paint the altarpiece but died in 1425. In completing it, Fra Angelico overcame the limitations inherent in the shape of the available surfaces by inventing a totally new kind of pictorial space. He employed his artistry, in accordance with the moral rules he followed both as a painter and as a profoundly committed religious man, in order to kindle feelings of devotion within the viewer that would bring him closer to the world of the divine.

It is true that in this composition, genuinely inspired though it is, we find a number of the features that appear in his earlier works: landscapes in the distance (cf. the *Lamentation*, fig. 58; the *San Marco Altarpiece*, fig. 67); angels on either side of the main subject (cf. the **Madonna**, in Frankfurt; the *Coronation of the Virgin*, in the Uffizi; the musician angels of the **Linaiuoli Triptych**, figs. 45 to 56; the *San Marco Altarpiece*, fig. 67); the central position of the main subject, with a magnifying effect that brings the subject closer and gives it a monumental quality; a deepening of the foreground, so as to increase the scope of our perception (cf. the San Marco Altarpiece, fig. 67; the Annalena Altarpiece, fig. 151; the Bosco ai Frati Altarpiece, fig. 153 — after his early works, Fra Angelico used this effect more and more often, more and more emphatically); and the use to which color is put, adding its own harmonics to the narrative movement of the scene.

But what is altogether new in this work — new for Fra Angelico and certainly new by comparison with the pictorial conventions of the time — is the way he has created and constructed space.

The composition is conceived in the shape of a broad V whose arms stretch out into the distance. He uses the three Gothic arches of the central panels like a wide-open gate giving onto the landscape; the three panels thus become a single panel, at the service of a single subject. This gateway — the upper portion aglow with golden foliage (and surmounted by the triangular pinnacles in which Fra Angelico left Lorenzo Monaco's three paintings untouched), the pilasters richly adorned with four quadrilobes and six panels depicting saints — is a great arch of glory; and within it we are given to read, with all the plastic quality of a Renaissance in progress, an extremely moving scene, a symphony of physical gestures, colors, prayers, and chanting choirs.

The musical strains of Ars Nova echo only remotely here; yet a certain profane polyphony remains, borne by the angels who fly over the site. If we were to take a strictly musical approach to this work, we might say that whereas the angels represent a style and content of singing which are already out of date, the work as a whole constitutes a new type of composition, full of resounding harmonies that produce a most moving and monumental masterpiece.

Why make this musical analogy? It was in 1443 that Fra Angelico undertook to paint the Santa Trinita Altarpiece, and it was almost a century later, in 1537, that Palestrina, then aged only twelve, began his life as a musician: he became a choir boy at the basilica of Santa Maria Maggiore in Rome. A century earlier in time and miles away (Rome was an almost distant province), Fra Angelico conceived — although in the form of painting — a music that broke completely with the conventions of his time, prefiguring the noble compositions of Palestrina, the great master of sacred music of the classical Italian Renaissance. A whole new phase of civilization, the dawn of our modern era, is typified in these two figures, each a genius in his own field but forged in the crucible of a common faith.

In this altarpiece, twenty figures are ranged around Jesus; a twenty-first figure weeps, half-hidden behind the group of men on the right, one of whom holds the three great nails (one for the feet, one for each hand) and the crown of thorns.

On the left, the group of holy women grieve for the dead Christ, while others prepare the shroud.

It is impossible to contemplate this scene without feeling our hearts beat faster, our faces flush with pity... But how can we speak about the unspeakable?

The branches of the V open out, extend into space like the "streets" which Palladio, in the next century, was to construct in his Teatro Olimpico in Vicenza, that crossroads of his architectural principles where so many works from antiquity were to be revived.

Here there is no fable, no borrowed element
Everything is timely,
everything essential.

At this very moment
they are dealing
with the dead man.

continued on page 290

fig. 131: Santa Trinita Altarpiece, c. 1443
Panel painting 176 × 185 cm

figs. 132, 133: Details from the Santa Trinita Altarpiece   figs. 134, 135: Details from the Santa Trinita Altarpiece

Santa Trinita Altarpiece
fig. 136: **A saint**
fig. 137: **An angel**
fig. 138: **St Peter**

Santa Trinita Altarpiece
fig. 139: **St Michael**
fig. 140: **St Francis**
fig. 141: **St Peter Martyr**

fig. 142: **St Andrew**

fig. 143: **St Paul**

fig. 144: San Giovanni
Gualberto

fig. 145: **St Dominic**

Their hands make folds in the flesh underneath
  his arms
while they lower
the large cadaver
as best they can.

How heavy he is
for the old man holding out his arms
to bear his weight! No one has ever
held such a burden of affliction before.

The ladders at the rear
are blotted from our sight
by bodies,
living and dead, that claim
our full attention. Like the man who
on the right weeps almost unseen,
the Cross bleeds
and stands silent
behind the bustle.

"Jesus of Nazareth, the King of the Jews"
  proclaims
the sign in Hebrew,
Greek and
Latin. No doubt about it, this is a
PUBLIC PLACE! We are all meant to know
WHO has been put to death.

In the distance,
flourishing gardens
lie just outside the walls of the wealthy
city. How bright the roof-tops are!
A cloud is moving on — has there been a
  storm?
If so, who in the town
remembers it?

The light is stark
and bright, slanting sideways,
a late-afternoon light.
In a little while
it will grow ruddy. But nothing shall be hidden.

The time has come to see.

figs. 146 to 148: **Details from the Santa Trinita Altarpiece**

290

Who would not care to see
in the distance over there,
to the right,
so sweet a landscape,
houses and castles climbing over hills.
Those tall and
reassuring trees,
rising
like fountains: a semblance
of a palm tree reminds us that it is surely hot,
in this Promised Land. The air's so
mild here.

The air lies
motionless on Jesus'
cheek — shadow lightly
hollows the top
of his shoulder and marks the collarbone.

The weight
of his head makes wrinkles
in the neck.

Beneath the eyelids
of a dead man, can the eyes
still see? The words of
love flow
from the closed mouth.

All upheaval ceases — the stilled eye
of the storm — the world is gathered together
in him, in this body, its skin
striped by the marks
of whiplashes.

Rivulets of blood
trickle slowly from the wounds
of sacrifice. With precision
they outline curves and hollows, and
on them mark
in vivid red
the end of pain.

fig. 149: **The Christ (Detail from the Santa Trinita Altarpiece)**
fig. 150: **Detail from the Santa Trinita Altarpiece**

294

When a great master whose work usually proceeds from inspiration carries out a stylistic exercise instead, the result is either out of phase or else surprising: out of phase and boring if the stylistic theories put into effect are used for their own sake, without the saving grace of innovation; surprising if the exercise is approached as a sort of game, acrobatics in which the goal is to leap over obstacles — or rather to make use of obstacles in order to derive from them a new type of impetus.

We agree with Pope-Hennessy that this Altarpiece (fig. 151) was executed after the one in San Marco (fig. 67) and that it should be dated 1443-45.

In the Annalena Altarpiece, Fra Angelico, as a painter of forms and resonances, carries his experiments to great lengths in accordance with the Renaissance spirit, and makes no reference to his beloved Gothic. He experiments with everything — the expression of architecture as construction; ornamentation; the use of colors, through daring chromatic juxtapositions.

He heaps up his effects: marble, fabrics, the fruit-and-garland motifs on the cornices, the contour of the throne, the sea-shell canopy of the niche, the two levels of the podium, the profusion of flowers and leaves in the foreground.

fig. 151: Annalena Altarpiece, 1443-5
Panel painting 180 × 202 cm

There are no landscapes such as we see in the San Marco Altarpiece; little expression in the faces of the participants; little movement; no dramatic narrative to tell us the why or the wherefore of this important gathering of saints (Peter Martyr, Cosmas, Damian, John the Evangelist, Lawrence, and Francis of Assisi) on either side of the Virgin and Child.

All of this might have proved quite abstract or lacking in interest, and far from commanding our admiration.

But as he worked on this altarpiece, Fra Angelico was transformed into an astonishing colorist and became caught up in his own game.

Into this somewhat overburdened and composite architectural setting (in which critics have detected the influences of a whole Areopagus of Tuscan geniuses, from Masaccio to Piero della Francesca, from Donatello to Luca della Robbia, elements borrowed directly from them, or even work carried out directly by their own hands), Fra Angelico injected a burst of colors and chromatic contrasts that transform a static construction and a stylistic exercise into a staggering masterpiece.

For once, the emotion contained in his work does not seem to come from its message of faith alone. It is produced by the purely sensual quality of the colors and forms, which come to life more miraculously, more intensely than in many other works by painters of the same period.

Using a device analogous to the score for the left hand which accompanies and merges with the melodic line in music, Fra Angelico stretches a broad band of gold — a length of brocade — across the painting, attaching the fabric to rings set between the arches of the marble wall in the background, just at or slightly above the top of the saints' haloes. Similar to the horizontal expanse of fabric in the San Marco Altarpiece, this hanging has,

however, a different function: it is not there to separate two worlds but to enhance the impact of the figures standing in front of it and to emphasize the intrinsic values of the upper portion of the painting, situated behind it.

Form for its own sake becomes a paean of praise unique in Fra Angelico's work.

The incredible pink tones punctuating this scene find their counterpart in the garments worn by John and the infant Jesus. Daring reds try to war with them, but there is no conflict after all;
it is resolved in a hymn of joy,
wherein gold gleams like citterns and cymbals.

In the foreground, the composition is symmetrically balanced by the sober homespun and sackcloth of the habits worn by the friar and the martyr. It is further set off by the broad black strip — the hand of God? — stretching across the top of the entire painting.

All is calm, all is peaceful in this interplay of varied elements; the artist is in perfect control.

What the painting achieves far exceeds this attempt to describe it; the whole is greater than the sum of its parts.

Through the perfection of forms which he attains, through his innovative powers — put to use for himself, therefore for us — Angelico speaks forcefully to us. We hear his voice, the voice of a man of prayer, in the midst of this silence.

And suddenly we look at this painting with different eyes.

The blue, now so light,
of Mary's great robe, with its deliberate folds,
sings a hymn of grace.
The child extends his hand a little awkwardly to caress his mother.
Their faces almost touch —
we witness the quintessence of tenderness.

fig. 152: Detail from the Annalena Altarpiece

fig. 153: **Bosco ai Frati Altarpiece, c. 1450-2**
Panel painting 200 × 174 cm

This work was carried out after 1450, when Fra Angelico had returned from Rome. It was commissioned by Cosimo de' Medici for the high altar of the Franciscan church in Bosco ai Frati, a small Tuscan village; Michelozzo had built the church a decade earlier. In dating this altarpiece, Pope-Hennessy points out the similarity between the style of the arches in the background and that of the arches in the Vatican fresco, the *Martyrdom of St Lawrence*, painted in approximately 1447-49. He also notes that the angels are handled in a way very similar to the handling of those on the ceiling at Orvieto, also painted around 1448.

Here we find no such provocative attempt to amplify space as we do in the *Coronation of the Virgin* (now in the Louvre) which dates from the same years.

Since the Bosco ai Frati Altarpiece (fig. 153), consisting of a large panel (1.75 m × 1.75 m), and its predella, is entirely by Fra Angelico's own hand, it constitutes for us his "classic" will and testament.

Noble groupings,
rhythmic harmonies,
balanced masses (of both figures and colors),
the full measure of inspiration.

fig. 154: Detail from the Bosco ai Frati Altarpiece
Virgin and Child

The subtle play of shadow on the niches and arches softens the edges of the architectural elements and suggests how gently the light slants into the scene from the side. Coming from the left, the light focuses on the face of an angel, far to the rear, and on the face of the Virgin, the radiant center of the work as a whole. The nude body of the infant Christ is modeled by the same soft light.

Here we find only half-tones of pink and red (except for the true reds of the hose and the hats on the right, which add timbre to the voices in this aria), while the browns and greens of some of the robes are answered by the blues and lavender of others.

The two trios of saints (Anthony of Padua, Louis of Toulouse, and Francis, on the left, fig. 158; Cosmas, Damian, and Peter Martyr, on the right, fig. 156) form corresponding and closely grouped masses and give the painting as a whole an almost anamorphic quality, attenuated by the bridging effect of the gold brocade fabric draped behind the Virgin. The angels' wings, of lighter gold, stand out against it, and in them we can make out a network of round peacock-feather eyes (figs. 159 and 160).

A cornice overlaid with imitation marble stretches across the top of the wall to the rear, on either side of the niche. Barely visible, scrollwork in the style of antiquity decorates the uprights above the niche, which disappear at the upper edge of the painting.

The floor in the foreground is seen from above; squares of marble, set in it as if they were small rugs (fig. 155), are an example of how decorative features can be used to enrich the contents of a scene. The handling of these squares is very subjective — the "veining" consists of cloudlike swirling shapes that seem to have been painted *al fresco*, by depositing scattered spots of color. They fill in a very

fig. 155: **Detail from the Bosco ai Frati Altarpiece**

spacious "forestage" and at the same time strengthen the affective tonality of the painting, a work of Fra Angelico's maturity.

To complete his plastic effect, Fra Angelico adds faint circles of pink and rose to the cheeks of the Virgin, the Child and St Cosmas; the touch is as light as if the color had been placed there by a caress.

Everything about this composition expresses tremendous tenderness (here, the faces of mother and child actually touch, fig. 154), conveying a warm, realistic impression of gentleness and intimacy.

There are prefigurations of Raphael, and also of Leonardo da Vinci, who was born in this very year, 1452. All of the faces with which we are familiar in Piero della Francesca's work are summed up in those of Saints Cosmas and Damian (fig. 156); they are strongly expressive, unlike the faces of the two divine figures.

Like a rivulet of water
springing from a rock,
green and gold
flow down the median border
of the Virgin's mantle,
source of life itself
within our grasp —
we need only reach for it.

We are all, in fact, all
symbolically present
within this work (no mere onlookers, we stand
　　inside it).
We, society,
in our primeval darkness
alive with murmurs, we
are embodied in the realm
of plant life shut off
from the warm world of belief
(remember the trees in the San Marco Altar-
　　piece, fig. 67, and in the *Noli Me Tangere*
　　fresco, the tufted trees beyond the enclosure
　　of the garden of the Sepulchre, fig. 72).

fig. 156: **St Cosmas, St Damian, St Peter Martyr**
Detail from the Bosco ai Frati Altarpiece

All the upper part of this Bosco ai Frati Altarpiece, on both sides of the shell-shaped canopy and behind it, is situated out of doors. We recognize the two palm trees (symbolizing death for the faith) alongside indeterminate species — ordinary mortals?

Society, not permitted to partake of the spiritual feast of communion with God.

This time, a communion such as this, totally symbolic, is entirely explicable. There is no question here of "filling in" space; an artist of Fra Angelico's stature never does so unless he can make the content and the process used integral parts of one another. What we are meant to perceive in this painting is a symbolic but clear warning to his time, which we, using the language of our own time, can interpret this way: *You may grasp the discoveries made by your contemporaries, but even as you adopt a philosophy of pragmatism, you must continually bear in mind that progress is not a matter of materialism alone.*

Fra Giovanni believed that the spiritual life was the real basis of human existence. Man had to shield and nurture his aspiration toward the divine (which today we tend to replace by, at best, a search for the absolute through an attempt to exceed our own limits) by practicing contemplation, which brings him nearer God.

Fra Angelico was like a man sworn to combat — religious combat. In an age of realism (the return to antiquity and the cult of the human being), he developed his painter's art, wherein beauty and emotion were only means by which to edify us — to stimulate us in turn to practice contemplation, to develop awareness of the sacred. His was a never-ending message.

As if to conclude, temporarily, this phase of his combat, Fra Angelico painted in the predella (along with six figures of saints) the most poignant dead Christ he ever conceived (fig. 157).

With this affecting Christ
he reminds us
that the source of all life
makes its way
through death, toward
its redemption.

Details from the Bosco ai Frati Altarpiece
fig. 157: The Dead Christ
fig. 158: St Anthony, St Louis of Toulouse, St Francis
figs. 159, 160: Two angels

The Scenes from the Life of Christ*

This extraordinary series of little paintings includes thirty-two panels (figs. 161 to 201), plus three others, painted by Baldovinetti (not reproduced here). Each panel measures 38.5 cm × 37 cm), except for the episode of the Last Judgment (fig. 199) which extends widthwise over two panels.

Since the series was intended to decorate the doors of the silver chest or cupboard containing offerings of the oratory of the Santissima Annunziata, construction of which was completed in 1451, these paintings can be dated approximately 1452-53.

They were later taken down, then reassembled in three groups. Starting with the *Raising of Lazarus* (fig. 176, the tenth panel, because we set aside those done by Baldovinetti), their attribution to Fra Angelico is very controversial, whereas all of the critics agree that the first nine panels (figs. 161 to 174) are by his hand and his only.

The current view with regard to the last twenty-three panels is that he probably took part in the preliminary drawings, but that the paintings themselves were executed by one or more artists who worked closely with Fra Angelico.

Each scene is explained by scrolls at top and bottom bearing relevant passages from the Old and New Testaments.

Early restorations caused some damage but have not altered the unity of the series.

We have decided to publish the entire series of thirty-two panels, for they are of undiminished interest as a unique cycle in which the narrative spirit of Fra Angelico's last period holds full sway, in a style freed of the weight of formal Gothic structures.

Wherever possible, we have transcribed the biblical quotations corresponding to the Latin inscriptions in the scrolls that appear in each scene.

We have preferred not to comment on these scenes, one by one, as we have done with the previous works. Instead, we leave the viewer to form his own impression of their beauty and unity. At this point in our exploration of Fra Angelico's development, each of us is in a position to establish for himself the appropriate correlation between the works we have already examined and these products of the master's greatest maturity.

* 1451-3 Panel paintings. Each panel is 38.5 × 37 cm except that of the *Last Judgment* n° 33 which is 38.5 × 74 cm.

319

Now it came to pass in the thirtieth year, in the fourth month, in the fifth day of the month, as I was among the captives by the river of Chebar, that the heavens were opened, and I saw visions of God. In the fifth day of the month, which was the fifth year of king Jehoiachin's captivity, The word of the Lord came expressly unto Ezekiel the priest, the son of Buzi, in the land of the Chaldeans by the river Chebar; and the hand of the Lord was there upon him.

And I looked, and, behold, a whirlwind came out of the north, a great cloud, and a fire infolding itself, and a brightness was about it, and out of the midst thereof as the colour of amber, out of the midst of the fire. Also out of the midst thereof came the likeness of four living creatures. And this was their appearance; they had the likeness of a man. And every one had four faces, and every one had four wings. And their feet were straight feet; and the sole of their feet was like the sole of a calf's foot: and they sparkled like the colour of burnished brass. And they had the hands of a man under their wings on their four sides; and they four had their faces and their wings. Their wings were joined one to another; they turned not when they went; they went every one straight forward. As for the likeness of their faces, they four had the face of a man, and the face of a lion, on the right side: and they four had the face of an ox on the left side; they four also had the face of an eagle. Thus were their faces: and their wings were stretched upward; two wings of every one were joined one to another, and two covered their bodies. And they went every one straight forward: whither the spirit was to go, they went; and they turned not when they went. As for the likeness of the living creatures, their appearance was like burning coals of fire, and like the appearance of lamps: it went up and down among the living creatures; and the fire was bright, and out of the fire went forth lightning. And the living creatures ran and returned as the appearance of a flash of lightning. Now as I beheld the living creatures, behold one wheel upon the earth by the living creatures, with his four faces. The appearance of the wheels and their work was like unto the colour of a beryl: and they four had one likeness: and their appearance and their work was as it were a wheel in the middle of a wheel.

Ezekiel 1, 1-16

fig. 161: Vision of Ezekiel (1)

Therefore the Lord himself shall give you a sign; Behold, a virgin shall conceive, and bear a son, and shall call his name Immanuel.

Isaiah 7, 14

fig. 162: **Detail from the Annunciation**

And in the sixth month the angel Gabriel was sent from God unto a city of Galilee, named Nazareth, To a virgin espoused to a man whose name was Joseph, of the house of David; and the virgin's name was Mary. And the angel came in unto her, and said, Hail, thou that art highly favoured, the Lord is with thee: blessed art thou among women. And when she saw him, she was troubled at his saying, and cast in her mind what manner of salutation this should be. And the angel said unto her, Fear not, Mary: for thou hast found favour with God. And, behold, thou shalt conceive in thy womb, and bring forth a son, and shalt call his name JESUS.

Luke 1, 26-31

ECCE VIRGO CONCIPIET 7 PARIET FILIVM 7 VOCABIT NOMEN EIVS EMANVL. YSA.VI.C

ECCE CONCIPIES INVTERO 7 PARIES FILIVM 7 VOCABIS NOMEN EI IHESVM .LVCE .I. C.

fig. 163: **Annunciation** (2)   fig. 164: **Detail from the Annunciation**

The people that walked in darkness have seen a great light: they that dwell in the land of the shadow of death, upon them hath the light shined. For unto us a child is born, unto us a son is given: and the government shall be upon his shoulder: and his name shall be called Wonderful, Counseller, The mighty God, The everlasting Father, The Prince of Peace.

Isaiah 9, 2-6

And so it was, that, while they were there, the days were accomplished that she should be delivered. And she brought forth her firstborn son, and wrapped him in swaddling clothes, and laid him in a manger; because there was no room for them in the inn.

Luke 2, 6-7

fig. 165: Nativity (3)

PARVVLVS NAT͂ Ē NOB͂ 7 FILI͂ DAT͂ Ē NOBIS 7 FACT͂ Ē PRINCIPAT͂ SVP HVMERṼ EI͂. YSA . IX . C .

͞MPLETI SVNT DIES VT PARERET 7 PEPERIT FILIVM SVVM PRIMOGENITVM . LVCE . II . C .

For thus saith the Lord to the men of Judah and Jerusalem, Break up your fallow ground, and sow not among thorns. Circumcise yourselves to the Lord, and take away the foreskins of your heart, ye men of Judah and inhabitants of Jerusalem: lest my fury come forth like fire, and burn that none can quench it, because of the evil of your doings.

Jeremiah 4, 3-4

And when eight days were accomplished for the circumcising of the child, his name was called JESUS, which was so named of the angel before he was conceived in the womb.

Luke 2, 21

fig. 166: Circumcision (4)

CIRCVCIDIMINI DOMINO VIRI IVDA 7 AVFERTE PPVTIA CORDIVM VESTRVM . IER . IIII . C .

POSTQVAB CONSVMATI SVNT DIES OCTO VT CIRCVCIDERET PVER VOCATV E NOM EI IHES . LVCE . II . C .

The kings of Tarshish and of the isles shall bring presents: the kings of Sheba and Seba shall offer gifts. Yea, all kings shall fall down before him: all nations shall serve him.

Psalms 72, 10-11

Now when Jesus was born in Bethlehem of Judæa, in the days of Herod the king, behold, there came wise men from the east to Jerusalem, Saying, Where is he that is born King of the Jews? for we have seen his star in the east, and are come to worship him.

And when they were come into the house, they saw the young child with Mary his mother, and fell down, and worshipped him: and when they had opened their treasures, they presented unto him gifts: gold, and frankincense, and myrrh.

Matthew 2, 1-2, 11

fig. 167: Adoration of the Magi (5)   fig. 168: Detail from the Adoration of the Magi

REGES TARSIS 7 INSVLE MVNERA OFFERET REGES ARABV 7 SABBA DONA ADVCET.PS. LXXI.C

ET APERTIS THESAVRIS SVIS OBTVLERVT EI AVRVM THVS 7 MIRRAM.MACEI.I.C.

Behold, I will send my messenger, and he shall prepare the way before me: and the Lord, whom ye seek, shall suddenly come to his temple, even the messenger of the covenant, whom ye delight in: behold, he shall come, saith the Lord of hosts.

Malachi 3, 1

And when the days of her purification according to the law of Moses were accomplished, they brought him to Jerusalem, to present him to the Lord; (As it is written in the law of the Lord, Every male that openeth the womb shall be called holy to the Lord;) And to offer a sacrifice according to that which is said in the law of the Lord, A pair of turtledoves, or two young pigeons.

Luke 2, 22-24

fig. 169: **Presentation in the Temple** (6)

STATIM VENIET AD TENPLŪ SACTŪ SVV DOMINATOR DN̅S Z ANGEL ESTAMETI QVE VOS VVLTIS. MAIACHI. II. C

TVLERV̄T IHESVM IN IERVSALEM VT DARENT OSTIAM PRO EO. LVCE. II. C.

And I said, Oh that I had wings like a dove! for then would I fly away, and be at rest.

Lo, then would I wander far off, and remain in the wilderness, Selah.

Psalms 55, 6-7

And when they were departed, behold, the angel of the Lord appeareth to Joseph in a dream, saying, Arise, and take the young child and his mother, and flee into Egypt, and be thou there until I bring thee word: for Herod will seek the young child to destroy him. When he arose, he took the young child and his mother by night, and departed into Egypt: and was there until the death of Herod: that it might be fulfilled which was spoken of the Lord by the prophet, saying, Out of Egypt have I called my son.

Matthew 2, 13-15

fig. 170: **D**etail from the **F**light into **E**gypt   fig. 171: **F**light into **E**gypt (7)

ELONGAVI FVGIENS 7 MANSI INSOLITVDINE . P̃S . XXXXXV . C

SVRGE ACCIPE PVERVM 7 MATREM EI͡9 7 FVGE INEGIPTVM . MACEI . II . C .

And it shall come to pass in that day, that the mountains shall drop down new wine, and the hills shall flow with milk, and all the rivers of Judah shall flow with waters, and a fountain shall come forth of the house of the Lord, and shall water the valley of Shittim. Egypt shall be a desolation, and Edom shall be a desolate wilderness, for the violence against the children of Judah, because they have shed innocent blood in their land.

Joel 3, 18-19

Then Herod, when he saw that he was mocked of the wise men, was exceeding wroth, and sent forth, and slew all the children that were in Bethlehem, and in all the coasts thereof, from two years old and under, according to the time which he had diligently inquired of the wise men.

Matthew 2, 16

fig. 172: **Detail from the Massacre of the Innocents**   fig. 173: **Massacre of the Innocents (8)**

NIQVE EGERVT INFILIOS IVDA EFVDERVT SANGVINE INOCENTE INTERRA SVA . IOLL . IIII . C

RATVS ERODES OCCIDIT OMNES PVEROS QVI ERAT INBETHELEHEM . MACEI . II . C

How do ye say, We are wise, and the law of the Lord is with us? Lo, certainly in vain made he it; the pen of the scribes is in vain. The wise men are ashamed, they are dismayed and taken: lo, they have rejected the word of the Lord; and what wisdom is in them?

Jeremiah 8, 8-9

And it came to pass, that after three days they found him in the temple, sitting in the midst of the doctors, both hearing them, and asking them questions. And all that heard him were astonished at his understanding and answers. And when they saw him, they were amazed: and his mother said unto him, Son, why hast thou thus dealt with us? behold, thy father and I have sought thee sorrowing. And he said unto them, How is it that ye sought me? wist ye not that I must be about my Father's business? And they understood not the saying which he spake unto them.

Luke 2, 46-50

fig. 174: Christ teaching in the Temple (9)

CÕFVSI SVT SAPIÊTES PTERRITI 7 CAPTI SVT SAPIENTIA NVLLA EST IN EIS . IERE . VIII . C

NVENERVT EV IN TEMPLO SEDENTÊ INMEDIO DOCTORV AVDIÊEM ILLOS 7 IÊROGAT . LVCE . II . C

DVCAM VOS DESEPVLCRIS POPVLVS MEVS. EÇECHIEL. XXXVII.C.
CLAMAVIT YHS VOCE MAG LAÇERE VENI FORAS. 7STATIM PRODIIT Q ERAT MORTVVS. IO. II. C.

Therefore prophesy and say unto them, Thus saith the Lord God; Behold, O my people, I will open your graves, and cause you to come up out of your graves, and bring you into the land of Israel. And ye shall know that I am the Lord, when I have opened your graves, O my people, and brought you up out of your graves. And shall put my spirit in you, and ye shall live, and I shall place you in your own land; then shall ye know that I the Lord have spoken it, and performed it, saith the Lord.

Ezekiel 37, 12-14

Now a certain man was sick, named Lazarus, of Bethany, the town of Mary and her sister Martha. (It was that Mary which anointed the Lord with ointment, and wiped his feet with her hair, whose brother Lazarus was sick). Therefore his sisters sent unto him, saying, Lord, behold, he whom thou lovest is sick.

Then when Jesus came, he found that he had lain in the grave four days already.

And when he thus had spoken, he cried with a loud voice, Lazarus, come forth. And he that was dead came forth, bound hand and foot with graveclothes; and his face was bound about with a napkin. Jesus saith unto them, Loose him, and let him go.

John 11, 1-3, 17, 43-44

fig. 175: **Detail from the Raising of Lazarus**

fig. 176: **Raising of Lazarus (13)**

Rejoice greatly, O daughter of Zion; shout, O daughter of Jerusalem: behold, thy King cometh unto thee: he is just, and having salvation; lowly, and riding upon an ass, and upon a colt the foal of an ass.

Zechariah 9, 9

And when they drew nigh unto Jerusalem, and were come to Bethphage, unto the mount of Olives, then sent Jesus two disciples. Saying unto them, Go into the village over against you, and straightway ye shall find an ass tied, and a colt with her: loose them, and bring them unto me.

And the disciples went, and did as Jesus commanded them. And brought the ass, and the colt, and put on them their clothes, and they set him thereon. And a very great multitude spread their garments in the way; others cut down branches from the trees, and strawed them in the way. And the multitudes that went before, and that followed, cried, saying, Hosanna to the Son of David: Blessed is he that cometh in the name of the Lord; Hosanna in the highest.

Matthew 21, 1-2, 6-9

fig. 177: Entry into Jerusalem (14)   fig. 178: Detail from the Entry into Jerusalem

CCE REX TVVS VENIT TIBI MANSVETVS SEDES SVP ASINA 7FILIV SVBIVGAL? ÇACHARÍ .IX.

OSANNA FILIO DAVID BENEDICTVS QVI VENIT IN NOMINE DOMINI . MACTEI . XXI.

AGNVM EIVSDEM ANNI INMACVLATVM FACIET SACRIFICIVM ЄÇECHIEL.XLVI.

PARAVERVNT PASCA 7CVM ESSET HORA DISCVBVIT YĤS 7DVODIM DISCIPVLI. LVCE .XXII. O

And in the feasts and in the solemnities the meat offering shall be an ephah to a bullock, and an ephah to a ram, and to the lambs as he is able to give, and an hin of oil to an ephah. Now when the prince shall prepare a voluntary burnt offering or peace offerings voluntarily unto the Lord, one shall then open him the gate that looketh toward the east, and he shall prepare his burnt offering and his peace offerings, as he did on the sabbath day: then he shall go forth; and after his going forth one shall shut the gate. Thou shalt daily prepare a burnt offering unto the Lord of a lamb of the first year without blemish: thou shalt prepare it every morning.

Ezekiel 46, 11-13

And when the hour was come, he sat down, and the twelve apostles with him. And he said unto them, With desire I have desired to eat this passover with you before I suffer: For I say unto you, I will not any more eat thereof, until it be fulfilled in the kingdom of God. And he took the cup, and gave thanks, and said, Take this, and divide it among yourselves: For I say unto you, I will not drink of the fruit of the vine, until the kingdom of God shall come. And he took bread, and gave thanks, and brake it, and gave unto them, saying, This is my body which is given for you: this do in remembrance of me. Likewise also the cup after supper, saying. This cup is the new testament in my blood, which is shed for you.

Luke 22, 14-20

fig. 179: **Last Supper** (15)

APPENDERVNT MERCEDEM MEAM TRIGINTA ARGENTEOS .ÇACHARIE .II. C.

OVID VVLTIS MICHI DARE 7 EGO TRADAM ILLVM . ATILLI COSTITVERVT FI XXX ARGEEOS . M . XXVI .

Thus saith the Lord my God; Feed the flock of the slaughter; Whose possessors slay them, and hold themselves not guilty: and they that sell them say, Blessed be the Lord; for I am rich: and their own shepherds pity them not. For I will no more pity the inhabitants of the land, saith the Lord: but, lo, I will deliver the men every one into his neighbour's hand, and into the hand of his king: and they shall smite the land, and out of their hand I will not deliver them. And I will feed the flock of slaughter, even you, O poor of the flock. And I took unto me two staves; the one I called Beauty and the other I called Bands; and I fed the flock. Three shepherds also I cut off in one month; and my soul lothed them, and their soul also abhorred me. Then said I, I will not feed you: that that dieth, let it die; and that that is to be cut off, let it be cut off; and let the rest eat every one the flesh of another. And I took my staff, even Beauty, and cut it asunder, that I might break my covenant which I had made with all the people. And it was broken in that day: and so the poor of the flock that waited upon me knew that it was the word of the Lord. And I said unto them, If ye think good, give me my price; and if not, forbear. So they weighed for my price thirty pieces of silver. And the Lord said unto me, Cast it unto the potter: a goodly price that I was prised at of them. And I took the thirty pieces of silver, and cast them to the potter in the house of the Lord. Then I cut asunder mine other staff, even Bands, that I might break the brotherhood between Judah and Israel.

Zechariah 11, 4-14

Then one of the twelve, called Judas Iscariot, went unto the chief priests. And said unto them, What will ye give me, and I will deliver him unto you? And they covenanted with him for thirty pieces of silver. And from that time he sought opportunity to betray him.

Matthew 26, 14-16

fig. 180: Judas Receiving Payment (16)   fig. 181: Detail from Judas Receiving Payment

Wash you, make you clean; put away the evil of your doings from before mine eyes; cease to do evil. Learn to do well; seek judgment, relieve the oppressed, judge the fatherless, plead for the widow.

Isaiah 1, 16-17

Now before the feast of the passover, when Jesus knew that his hour was come that he should depart out of this world unto the Father, having loved his own which were in the world, he loved them unto the end. And supper being ended, the devil having now put into the heart of Judas Iscariot, Simon's son, to betray him; Jesus knowing that the Father had given all things into his hands, and that he was come from God, and went to God; He riseth from supper, and laid aside his garments; and took a towel, and girded himself. After that he poureth water into a bason, and began to wash the disciples' feet, and to wipe them with the towel wherewith he was girded.

John 13, 1-5

fig. 182: Christ Washing the Feet of the Apostles (17)

LAVAMINI MVNDI ESTOE AVFERE MALVM COGITATIONVM VESTRARVM. ISAIE. I. C.

MISIT AQVĀ INPELVIM 7CEPIT LAVARE PEDES DISCIPVLORVM 7EXERGERE LĪ IEO. IO. XIII. C

And, thou son of man, thus saith the Lord God; Speak unto every feathered fowl, and to every beast of the field, Assemble yourselves, and come; gather yourselves on every side to my sacrifice that I do sacrifice for you, even a great sacrifice upon the mountains of Israel, that ye may eat flesh, and drink blood.

Ezekiel 39, 17

The Jews therefore strove among themselves, saying, How can this man give us his flesh to eat? Then Jesus said unto them, Verily, verily, I say unto you, Except ye eat the flesh of the Son of man, and drink his blood, ye have no life in you. Whoso eateth my flesh, and drinketh my blood, hath eternal life; and I will raise him up at the last day.

John 6, 52-54

fig. 183: Institution of the Eucharist (18)

Fear thou not; for I am with thee: be not dismayed; for I am thy God: I will strengthen thee; yea, I will help thee; yea, I will uphold thee with the right hand of my righteousness.

Behold, all they that were incensed against thee shall be ashamed and confounded: they shall be as nothing; and they that strive with thee shall perish.

Isaiah 41, 10-11

And he came out, and went, as he was wont, to the mount of Olives; and his disciples also followed him. And when he was at the place, he said unto them, Pray that ye enter not into temptation. And he was withdrawn from them about a stone's cast, and kneeled down, and prayed, Saying, Father, if thou be willing, remove this cup from me: nevertheless not my will, but thine, be done. And there appeared an angel unto him from heaven, strengthening him.

Luke 22, 39-43

fig. 184: Agony in the Garden (19)

NE TIMEA QVIA TECV SVM EGO DEVS CONFORTAVI TE . YSAIE . XXXXI . C

APPARVIT AT EI ANGELVS DECEL CONFORTANS EVM . LVCE . XXII . C

All that hate me whisper together against me: against me do they devise my hurt.

An evil disease, say they, cleaveth fast unto him: and now that he lieth he shall rise up no more.

Yea, mine own familiar friend, in whom I trusted, which did eat of my bread, hath lifted up his heel against me.

Psalms 41, 7-9

And while he yet spake, lo, Judas, one of the twelve, came, and with him a great multitude with swords and staves, from the chief priests and elders of the people. Now he that betrayed him gave them a sign, saying, Whomsoever I shall kiss, that same is he: hold him fast. And forthwith he came to Jesus, and said, Hail, master; and kissed him. And Jesus said unto him, Friend, wherefore art thou come? Then came they, and laid hands on Jesus, and took him.

Matthew 26, 47-50

fig. 185: Betrayal of Christ (20)   fig. 186: Detail from the Betrayal of Christ

QVI EDEBAT PANES MEOS MAGNIFICAVIT SVP ME SVPPLATATOEM . PS . XL .

ET CŌFESTIM ACCEDĒS IVDAS AD XPM DIXIT AVE RABBI . ZOSTVLATVS Ē EV. MXXVI.

QVI EDEBAT PANES MEOS MAGNIFICAVIT

But thou, O son of man, behold, they shall put bands upon thee, and shall bind thee with them, and thou shalt not go out among them.

Ezekiel 3, 25

And while he yet spake, lo, Judas, one of the twelve, came, and with him a great multitude with swords and staves, from the chief priests and elders of the people. Now he that betrayed him gave them a sign, saying, Whomsoever I shall kiss, that same is he: hold him fast. And forthwith he came to Jesus, and said, Hail, master; and kissed him. And Jesus said unto him, Friend, wherefore art thou come? Then came they, and laid hands on Jesus, and took him.

Matthew 26, 47-50

fig. 187: Arrest of Christ (21)

ECCE DATA SVNT SVPER TE VINCVLA ET LIGABVNT TE IN EIS . EZECHIEL . III . C .

AT ILLI TENĒTES YHM DVXERVT EV LIGATV ADCHAIPHAN PNCIPE IVDEORV M XX VII C

But thou, Bethlehem Ephratah, though thou be little among the thousands of Judah, yet out of thee shall he come forth unto me that is to be ruler un Israel; whose goings forth have been from old, from everlasting.

Micah 5, 2

Then led they Jesus from Caiaphas unto the hall of judgment: and it was early; and they themselves went not into the judgment hall, lest they should be defiled; but that they might eat the passover. Pilate then went out unto them, and said, What accusation bring ye against this man? They answered and said unto him, If he were not a malefactor, we would not have delivered him up unto thee. Then said Pilate unto them, Take ye him, and judge him according to your law. The Jews therefore said unto him, It is not lawful for us to put any man to death. That the saying of Jesus might be fulfilled, which he spake, signifying what death he should die. Then Pilate entered into the judgment hall again, and called Jesus, and said unto him, Art thou the King of the Jews? Jesus answered him, Sayest thou this thing of thyself, or did others tell it thee of me? Pilate answered, Am I a Jew? Thine own nation and the chief priests have delivered thee unto me: what hast thou done? Jesus answered, My kingdom is not of this world: if my kingdom were of this world, then would my servants fight, that I should not be delivered to the Jews: but now is my kingdom not from hence.

John 18, 28-36

fig. 188: Christ before Caiaphas (22)

PERCVTIENT MAXILLAM IVDICIS ISRL. MICHEE . V . C .

ASSISTES MINISTRORV DEDIT ALAPA VHM DICES SIC RESPODES PONTIFICI . IO . XVIII.

And the men that held Jesus mocked him, and smote him, And when they had blindfolded him, they struck him on the face, and asked him, saying, Prophesy, who is it that smote thee? And many other things blasphemously spake they against him.

Luke 22, 63-65

And now, O inhabitants of Jerusalem, and men of Judah, judge, I pray you, betwixt me and my vineyard. What could have been done more to my vineyard, that I have not done in it? wherefore, when I looked that it should bring forth grapes, brought it forth wild grapes?

Isaiah 5, 3-4

fig. 189: **Mocking of Christ** (23)

FACIEM M̄ȲI̅ Ñ AŪTI ABSCREPĀTIB̄ ⁊ CŌSPVĒTIB̄ ĪME. ISAIE . V . C.

LLVDEBANT EI CEDENTES ⁊ VELAVERVNT FACIEM EIVS. LVCE. XXII. C

When the wicked, even mine enemies and my foes, came upon me to eat up my flesh, they stumbled and fell.

Psalms 27, 2

*Then **Pilate** therefore took **Jesus**, and scourged him. And the soldiers platted a crown of thorns, and put it on his head, and they put on him a purple robe, And said, Hail, **King** of the **Jews!** and they smote him with their hands.*

John 19, 1-3

fig. 190: Flagellation (24)

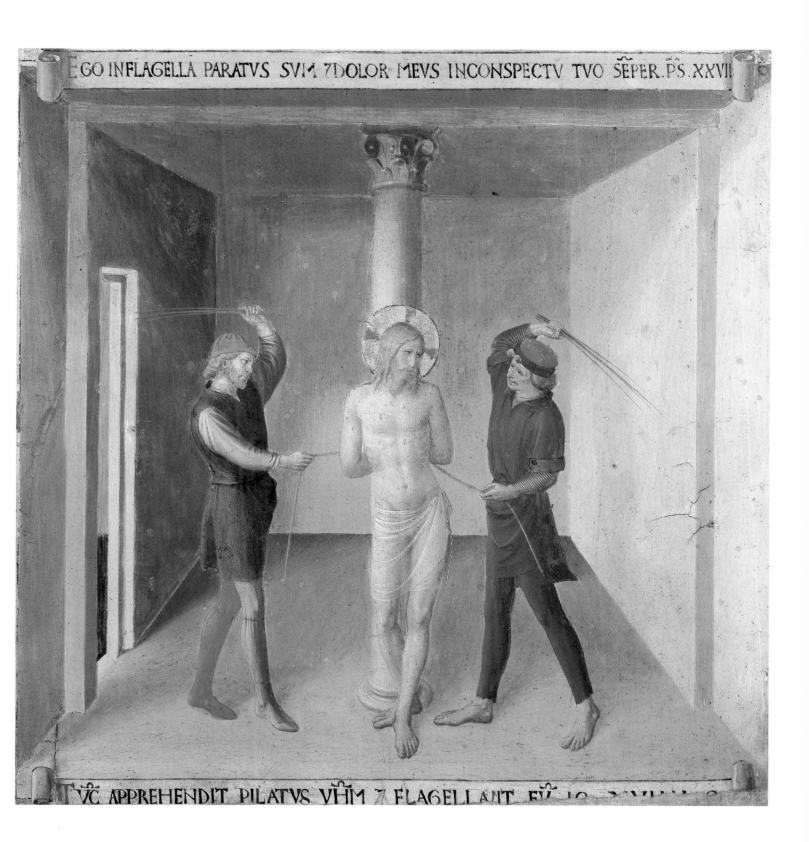

EGO IN FLAGELLA PARATVS SVM 7 DOLOR MEVS IN CONSPECTV TVO SẼPER. PS. XXVII

TV̄C APPREHENDIT PILATVS VH̄M 7 FLAGELLAVT EV̄ IO̅ XVIII

All we like sheep have gone astray; we have turned every one to his own way; and the Lord hath laid on him the iniquity of us all. He was oppressed, and he was afflicted, yet he opened not his mouth: he is brought as a lamb to the slaughter, and as a sheep before her shearers is dumb, so he openeth not his mouth.

Isaiah 53, 6-7

And as they led him away, they laid hold upon one Simon, a Cyrenian, coming out of the country, and on him they laid the cross, that he might bear it after Jesus. And there followed him a great company of people, and of women which also bewailed and lamented him.

Luke 23, 26-27

fig. 191: Christ Carrying the Cross (25)

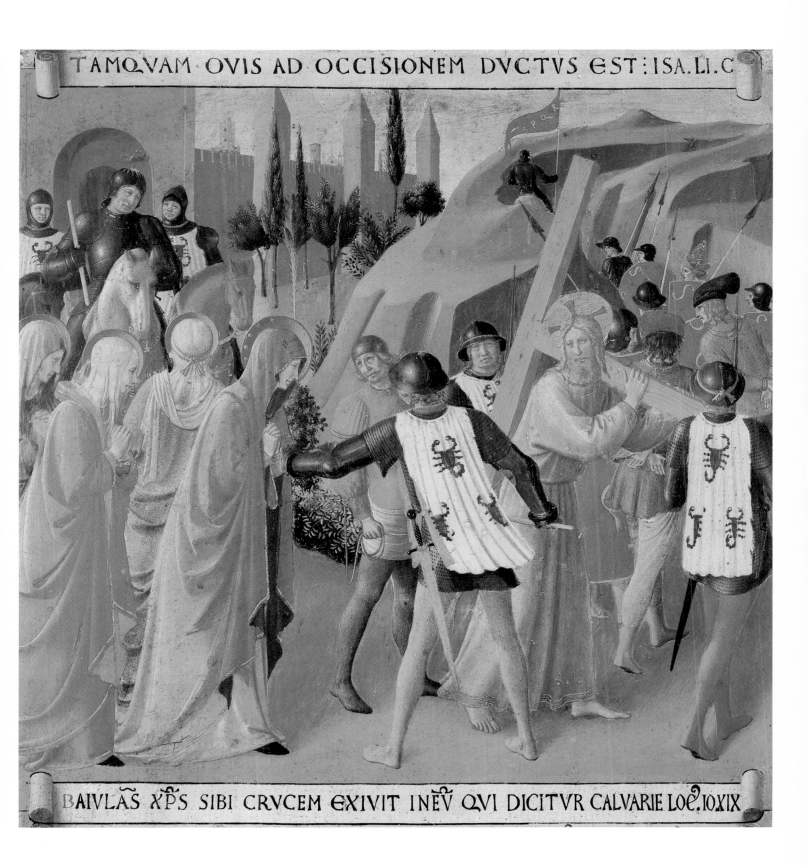

TAMQVAM OVIS AD OCCISIONEM DVCTVS EST:ISA.LI.C

BAIVLÃS XPS SIBI CRVCEM EXIVIT INEV QVI DICITVR CALVARIE LOC̃.IOXIX

I may tell all my bones: they look and stare upon me.
They part my garments among them, and cast lots upon my vesture.

Psalms **22**, 17-18

And after that they had mocked him, they took the robe off from him, and put his own raiment on him, and led him away to crucify him.

And they crucified him, and parted his garments, casting lots: that it might be fulfilled which was spoken by the prophet, They parted my garments among them, and upon my vesture did they cast lots.

Matthew **27**, 31-35

fig. 192: **S**tripping of **C**hrist (26)

DIVISERVT SIBI VESTIMENTA MEA 7 SVPER VESEM MEA MISERVT SORE. PS. XXI.

DIVISERVNT MILITES VESTIMETA EIVS SORTEM MICTENTES . M. XXVI. C.

Surely he hath borne our griefs, and carried our sorrows: yet we did esteem him stricken, smitten of God, and afflicted. But he was wounded for our transgressions, he was bruised for our iniquities: the chastisement of our peace was upon him; and with his stripes we are healed.

Isaiah 53, 4-5

And when they were come unto a place called Golgotha, that is to say, a place of a skull, They gave him vinegar to drink mingled witth gall: and when he had tasted thereof, he would not drink.

And they crucified him, and parted his garments, casting lots: that it might be fulfilled which was spoken by the prophet, They parted my garments among them, and upon my vesture did they cast lots. And sitting down they watched him there; And set up over his head his accusation written, THIS IS JESUS THE KING OF THE JEWS.
Then were there two thieves crucified with him, one on the right hand, and another on the left.

Matthew 27, 33-38

fig. 193: Crucifixion (27)

And he made his grave with the wicked, and with the rich in his death; because he had done no violence, neither was any deceit in his mouth.

Isaiah 53, 9

When the even was come, there came a rich man of Arimathæa, named Joseph, who also himself was Jesus' disciple: He went to Pilate, and begged the body of Jesus. Then Pilate commanded the body to be delivered. And when Joseph had taken the body, he wrapped it in a clean linen cloth, And laid it in his own new tomb, which he had hewn out in the rock: and he rolled a great stone to the door of the sepulchre, and departed. And there was Mary Magdalene, and the other Mary, sitting over against the sepulchre.

Matthew 27, 57-61

fig. 194: Lamentation (28)

PM GENTES DEPRECABVT R 7 ERIT SEPVLCRVM EIVS GLORIOSVM. YS. XI:

IOSEPH DEPOSITŪ CORPVS IHV I VOLVIT IN SINDONE 7 POSVIT IN MONVMĒTO. LV. XXIII.

Then they cried unto the Lord in their trouble, and he saved them out of their distresses. He brought them out of darkness and the shadow of death, and brake their bands in sunder.

Psalms 107, 13-14

And I beheld, and, lo, in the midst of the throne and of the four beasts, and in the midst of the elders, stood a Lamb as it had been slain, having seven horns and seven eyes, which are the seven Spirits of God sent forth into all the earth. And he came and took the book out of the right hand of him that sat upon the throne. And when he had taken the book, the four beasts and four and twenty elders fell down before the Lamb, having every one of them harps, and golden vials full of odours, which are the prayers of saints. And they sung a new song, saying, Thou art worthy to take the book, and to open the seals thereof: for thou wast slain, and hast redeemed us to God by thy blood out of every kindred, and tongue, and people, and nation; And hast made us unto our God kings and priests: and we shall reign on the earth.

Revelation 5, 6-10

fig. 195: Christ in Limbo (29)

In the end of the sabbath, as it began to dawn toward the first day of the week, came Mary Magdalene and the other Mary to see the sepulchre. And, behold, there was a great earthquake: for the angel of the Lord descended from heaven, and came and rolled back the stone from the door, and sat upon it. His countenance was like lightning, and his raiment white as snow: And for fear of him the keepers did shake, and became as dead men. And the angel answered and said unto the women, Fear not ye: for I know that ye seek Jesus, which was crucified. He is not here: for he is risen, as he said. Come, see the place where the Lord lay. And go quickly, and tell his disciples that he is risen from the dead; and, behold, he goeth before you into Galilee; there shall ye see him: lo, I have told you.

Matthew 28, 1-7

fig. 196: **The Marys at the Sepulchre** (30)

In my distress I called upon the Lord, and cried unto my God: he heard my voice out of his temple, and my cry came before him, even, into his ears.

Then the earth shook and trembled; the foundations also of the hills moved and were shaken, because he was wroth. There went up a smoke out of his nostrils, and fire out of his mouth devoured: coals were kindled by it.

He bowed the heavens also, and came down: and darkness was under his feet.

And he rode upon a cherub, and did fly: yea, he did fly upon the wings of the wind.

Psalms 18, 6-10

And he led them out as far as to Bethany, and he lifted up his hands, and blessed them. And it came to pass, while he blessed them, he was parted from them, and carried up into heaven.

Luke 24, 50-51

fig. 197: **Ascension** (31)

SCĒDIT SVP CELOS ⁊VOLAVIT SVP PEÑAS VENTORVM·PŜ·XVII·C~

DÑS YĤVS POSTŌ̃LOCVTVS Ē AŜSV̄TVS Ē ĨCELVM·M̂·VLTIMO

Be glad then, ye children of Zion, and rejoice in the Lord your God: for he hath given you the former rain moderately, and he will cause to come down for you the rain, the former rain, and the latter rain in the first month.

Joel 2, 23

And when the day of Pentecost was fully come, they were all with one accord in one place. And suddenly there came a sound from heaven as of a rushing mighty wind, and it filled all the house where they were sitting. And there appeared unto them cloven tongues like as of fire, and it sat upon each of them.

Acts 2, 1-3

fig. 198: Pentecost (32)

Every way of a man is right in his own eyes: but the Lord pondereth the hearts.

It is joy to the just to do judgment: but destruction shall be to the workers of iniquity. The man that wandereth out of the way of understanding shall remain in the congregation of the dead.

Proverbs 21, 2, 15-16

When the Son of man shall come in his glory, and all the holy angels with him, then shall he sit upon the throne of his glory: And before him shall be gathered all nations: and he shall separate them one from another, as a shepherd divideth his sheep from the goats: And he shall set the sheep on his right hand, but the goats on the left. Then shall the King say unto them on his right hand, Come, ye blessed of my Father, inherit the kingdom prepared for you from the foundation of the world: For I was an hungred, and ye gave me meat: I was thirsty, and ye gave me drink: I was a stranger, and ye took me in: Naked, and ye clothed me: I was sick, and ye visited me: I was in prison, and ye came unto me. Then shall the righteous answer him, saying, Lord, when saw we thee an hungred, and fed thee? or thirsty, and gave thee drink? When saw we thee a stranger, and took thee in? or naked, and clothed thee? Or when saw we thee sick, or in prison, and came unto thee? And the King shall answer and say unto them, Verily I say unto you, Inasmuch as ye have done it unto one of the least of these my brethren, ye have done it unto me.

Then shall he say also unto them on the left hand, Depart from me, ye cursed, into everlasting fire, prepared for the devil and his angels: For I was an hungred, and ye gave me no meat: I was thirsty, and ye gave me no drink: I was a stranger, and ye took me not in: naked, and ye clothed me not: sick, and in prison, and ye visited me not.

Matthew 25, 31-43

fig. 199: Last Judgment (33)

SCĒDĀT GĒTES ĪVALLĒ IOSAPHT QᴏA IBI SEDEBO VT IVDICE OMS ĜTES IOE · SEDEBIT SVᴘ SEDᴇ ᴍAIESTATIS SVE 7IVDICᴇBIT BOIIS ᴜMALOˢ · Ⓜ · XXV · Ⓒ

VENITE BENEDICTI PATRIS MEI RCIPITE REGNVM · Ⓜ · XXV · Ⓒ   ITE MALEDICTI TIGNIEM ETERNVM · Ⓜ · XXV · Ⓒ

Thou shalt also be a crown of glory in the hand of the Lord, and a royal diadem in the hand of thy God.

Thou shalt no more be termed Forsaken; neither shall thy land any more be termed Desolate: but thou shalt be called Hephzibah, and thy land Beulah: for the Lord delighteth in thee, and thy land shall be married.

Isaiah 62, 3-4

fig. 200: Coronation of the Virgin (34)

IDI DÑM SEDÉ͂EM SVPER SOLIV̄ EXCELSV̄ 7 ELEVATVM 7 PLENA DOM͂ MAIESTAE EI͂. YSA.VI

CCE TABERNACVLV̄ DEI CV̄ HOÍNIB͂ 7 HĪTABIT CV̄ EIS 7 IPI PPL̄S EI͂ ERV̄T 7 IP̄E D̄S EORV̄.APOCLXXI

Selected Bibliography

P. d'Ancona, *Beato Angelico*, Milan, 1953

G. C. Argan, *Fra Angelico*, Geneva, 1955.

U. Baldini, « Commentari », 1956.
Beato Angelico, Bergamo, 1964.
L'Opera completa dell'Angelico, Milan, 1970.
Fra Angelico, Flammarion, Paris, 1973.

G. Bazin, *Fra Angelico*, New York 1941, Paris, 1949.

B. Berenson, *The Florentine Painters of the Renaissance*, New York - London, 1896.
The Italian Pictures of the Renaissance : Florentine School, Oxford, 1932 and London, 1963.
The Drawings of the Florentine Painters, Chicago, 1938, 1970.

L. Berti - U. Baldini, *Catalogo della Mostra delle opere del Beato Angelico*, Florence-Rome, 1955.

L. Berti, « Bollettino d'arte », 1962.
« Acropoli », IV 1962, I 1963.
Angelico, Florence, 1967.
Il Museo di San Marco in Firenze, Milan, 1961.

L. Berti - B. Bellardoni - E. Battisti, *Angelico a San Marco*, Rome, 1966.

L. Collobi Ragghianti, « Critica d'arte », VII 1950, IX 1955.

A. M. Francini Ciaranfi, *Beato Angelico, Gli affreschi di San Marco a Firenze*, Milan, 1947.

S. Frosali, *L'Angelico*, Florence 1965.

M. L. Gengaro, *Il Beato Angelico a San Marco*, Bergamo, 1944.

R. Huyghe, *Fra Angelico*, Paris, 1966.

A. Jahn-Rusconi, *Il Museo di San Marco a Firenze*, Milan, 1950.
Mostra delle opere del Beato Angelico (catalogue), Florence, 1955.

R. Langton Douglas, *Fra Angelico*, London, 1911.

P. V. Marchese, *Memorie dei più insigni pittori, scultori e architetti domenicani*, Florence, 1845-54, Bologna, 1878.

U. Middeldorf, « Rinascimento », 1937, 1955.

P. Muratoff, *Frate Angelico*, Rome, 1930.

S. Orlandi, *Beato Angelico*, Florence, 1964.
« Rivista d'arte », 1954.
« Memorie domenicane », 1955.
Sant'Antonino, Florence, 1959-60.

A. Pichon, *Fra Angelico*, Paris, 1922.

J. Pope-Hennesy, *Fra Angelico*, London, 1952.
Angelico, Florence, 1985.

U. Procacci, *Catalogo della Mostra dei documenti sulla vita e le opere dell'Angelico e delle fonti storiche fino al Vasari*, Florence, 1955.

R. Rapini, *Fra Giovanni Angelico*, Bologna, 1925.

F. Rondoni, *Guida del Museo Fiorentino di San Marco*, Florence, 1872.

M. Salmi, *Il Beato Angelico*, Milan, 1958.

F. Schottmüller, *Fra Angelico : des Meisters Gemälde*, Stuttgart, 1924.

E. Schneider, *Fra Angelico da Fiesole*, Paris, 1924, 1933.

G. Sinibaldi, *Il Museo di San Marco di Firenze*, Rome, 1936.

G. Urbani, *Il Beato Angelico*, Milan, 1957.
Angelico, « Enciclopedia universale dell'arte », I, Venice-Rome, 1958.

R. Van Marle, *The Development of the Italian Schools of Painting*, X, the Hague, 1928.

A. Wurm, *Meister-und Schularbeit in Fra Angelicos Werk*, Strasbourg, 1907.

Index

Photographic Credits : Studio fotografico Nicolò Orsi Battaglini, Florence.

PRINTED BY
MONDADORI, VERONA
WITH THE COLLABORATION OF
MONDGRAPH, PARIS